not your beading
mama's™

not your mama's™ beading

The cool and creative way to string 'em along

by Kate Shoup Welsh

Wiley Publishing, Inc.

Published by Wiley Publishing, Inc., Hoboken, New Jersey

For general information on our other products and services or to obtain technical support please contact our Customer Care Department within the U.S. at (800) 762-2974, outside the U.S. at (317) 572-3993 or fax (317) 572-4002.

Wiley also publishes its books in a variety of electronic formats. Some content that appears in print may not be available in electronic books. For more information about Wiley products, please visit our web site at www.wiley.com.

Library of Congress Cataloging-in-Publication data is available from the publisher upon request.

ISBN-13 978-0-471-97380-5
ISBN-10 0-471-97380-7

Printed in the United States of America

10 9 8 7 6 5 4 3 2 1

Book design by Elizabeth Brooks
Cover design by Troy Cummings
Interior photography by Matt Bowen
Illustrations by Shelley Norris and Joni Burns
Book production by Wiley Publishing, Inc. Composition Services

For Jackie

Free bonus pattern available online!

Can't get enough beading? Access one more *Not Your Mama's Beading* pattern at www.wiley.com/go/NYMbeading.

Contents

Acknowledgments

No project that is the size and scope of a book can be completed without the help of many, *many* others. For this book, much credit is due to Cindy Kitchel, whose talents as a publisher are exceeded only by her talents as a friend. Roxane Cerda, my acquisitions editor, was exceedingly patient and kind, even when I was more trouble than I was worth. Project editor Donna Wright's encouragement and suggestions throughout the book-writing process proved invaluable. And Elizabeth Kim, the book's copy editor, saved my proverbial ass on numerous occasions. Thanks are also due to Christina Stambaugh, who provided design direction, Elizabeth Brooks, who designed and laid out the book; Sossity Smith, who proofread it; and Kevin Broccoli, who indexed it.

Then, of course, there are those people who had the unfortunate luck to live with or otherwise encounter me during the writing process: my amazing and supportive husband, Ian, who never fails to make me feel beautiful, smart, and funny, even at times when I am none of the above; my gorgeous, brilliant, and hilarious five-year-old daughter, Heidi, who already knows how to correctly use the word "scatological" in a sentence (and, our views on etiquette being what they are, has frequent cause); my mom, Barb Shoup, who was a writer long before I was and has the resume and awards to prove it; my dad, Steve Shoup, whose encouraging words (specifically, "Who the hell wants to read about beading?!") won't soon be forgotten; and my sister, Jenny Shoup, who, in addition to being a mom, a wife, a dancer, and a writer *also* manages to work full time as an attorney *and* hang out with me. I love you all more than I can say.

Introduction

◆◆◆

Beadginning Remarks

Beadaholics Anonymous

What do Lisa Kudrow, Kate Hudson, Mira Sorvino, Jennifer Tilly, and Cher have in common? Yes, they're all actresses, that's a given. And, okay, you're right—nudie photos of each of these women are available online. That's not my point. What I'm getting at is that all five of these ladies are beaders.

Of course, Lisa, Kate, Mira, Jennifer, and Cher aren't the only ones on the beading bandwagon. In the last 5 years, beading—formerly the domain of women who a) collected Precious Moments figurines, b) wore appliquéd sweatshirts, c) just couldn't see why Thelma and Louise had to die at the end, or d) all of the above—has exploded into a $1.5-billion business in the U.S. Not convinced? Type "beading" into any search engine box, and you'll net nearly 2,700,000 hits.

Considering that beading has been around since Neanderthals roamed Earth (and I mean *actual* Neanderthals, not your ex-boyfriend), you have to wonder: Why now? What could explain this surge in beading in the United States—indeed, this surge in nearly all types of crafts, from knitting to sewing and beyond (although not, I'm guessing, those little latch-hooky rugs, circa 1978, which usually featured a picture of an owl, of flowers, or of Woodstock from *Peanuts*)? Some believe that this resurgence in the "womanly arts" (barf) is a direct result of the events of September 11, 2001. That is, the terrorist attacks on that day understandably made Americans a bit travel shy, which meant they had more time for home-based hobbies. (Supporting this "if you don't bead, the terrorists win" view is the fact that one bead store in Washington state actually sold out of red, white, and blue beads in the aftermath of 9/11.) Others suggest that the increase in craft hobbyists stems from the void that is modern life—the implication being that making things with our own hands reconnects us with our, well, Neanderthal selves. (No offense.) The lousy economy hasn't hurt either; do-it-yourself types can create extremely nice jewelry for much less than comparable store-bought pieces. And of course, there's the never-ending quest to wear something unique, something that your obnoxious, brown-nosing cube-mate can only covet.

For whatever reason, there's no doubt about it: Beading has become *cool*. And like many other cool things—illicit drugs come to mind (not that I'm endorsing them, of course)—beading is also addictive. For one, beads are shiny, and anyone who's anyone knows that handling shiny objects is habit-forming. Plus, beading provides an immediate rush. Forget knitting. Making a single sweater can take longer than growing your pixie haircut into a *Maxim* babe's mane. With beading, you can crank out any number of trinkets in the time it takes to pluck your mustache. And of course, although certain beading techniques do require some skill, it's possible to make many beautiful pieces armed only with the ability to poke thread through a bead. To sum things up, if you like shiny things, have the attention span of cotton, and possess opposable thumbs, beading is the hobby for you.

How This Book Is Organized

If you've opened this book, I'm assuming you're interested in learning more about beading. Either that or the bookshop stacks you were perusing just fell on you, and this is the only book you could reach while awaiting rescue. Either way, this book is designed to get you up and running. (Whoa—not *actual* running, thank God.) The first part starts with a brief history of beading, the upshot of which is that your slavish devotion to personal adornment is the result not of greed or of vanity but rather of thousands of years of evolution, and is therefore excusable. From there, you'll discover the various tools and materials that no beader should bead without. Put another—perhaps more compelling—way, you'll find out what you get to buy. Then it's on to a discussion of various beading techniques, including stringing, stitching, knotting, and wirework. As you'll quickly learn, beading can be as simple—or as complex—as you want it to be. Kind of like a Starbucks order.

With those skills under your belt, you're ready for Part Two: the projects. Here you'll find 34 designs for necklaces, bracelets, rings, earrings, accessories, and home decor items. Each project contains step-by-step instructions, a list of the materials you'll need, an estimate of how much those materials will cost, and a ballpark figure of the level of commitment required to complete the design. You'll be able to complete projects described as "Flirtation" in less time than it takes to paint your toes; "Love o' Your Life" projects, in contrast, will take you longer to finish, but will result in heirloom-quality pieces (unless you botch them up—again, no judgment); a project categorized as a "Fling" falls somewhere in between. (Notice that no projects are tagged "Six Post-Breakup Months Stalking Your Ex." No judgment. Well, maybe a little.) Finally, the appendixes in the back of the book provide some handy beading resources.

Whatever, Little Miss Know-It-All

If you're already a seasoned beader, I'm guessing you can safely skip the first part of this book, but I should inform you that sections of it are deeply funny. I mean, I think so anyway. Or maybe they're not. Whatever. Look, all I'm saying is, if you've strung a bead or two in your day and you want to dive straight into the projects, by all means, have at it. If, however, you're new to this whole beading thing, I urge you to read Part One before moving forward. But, I mean, it's up to you. Seriously. No judgment.

Who This Book Is For

If you've never strung a bead, let alone made a right-angle weave bracelet, this book is for you. In its pages, you'll discover what tools you need to buy, what materials are available, and the techniques you'll need to develop to make store-worthy pieces. That's not to say, however, that if you're an intermediate or even an advanced beader, you won't enjoy this book—especially Part Two, "Projects." With designs ranging from the ridiculously simple to the sublimely complex, there really is something for everyone.

Well, okay, maybe not *everyone*. This is, after all, *Not Your Mama's Beading.* That means if you in any way resemble *Whistler's Mother*, you probably won't be interested in this book. If you have hosted a Tupperware party without feeling at least a little bit embarrassed, this may not be the book for you. If you willingly watch *Yanni: Live at the Acropolis,* you might want to move on down the shelf. But if you're cool, you're hip, and you want to learn how to make some kick-ass beaded pieces, read on.

· Part One ·

Brushing Up on Beading

Chapter One

◆◆◆

Beads in Our Time

Given the early hominid's love affair with the bead, you might reasonably conclude that *my* beading instincts—the ones that provoked me to buy a bundle of fabulous Swarovski crystals in lieu of making my credit card payment— are the result of 40 millennia of evolution, as much a product of my DNA as my hair color (before it was highlighted, that is). Whether this is in fact true remains to be seen, but it certainly sounds adequately scientific to hold water in the event my spouse questions my "excessive" beading-related purchases. In case you find yourself being cross-examined about your beading, this chapter contains enough historical information to snow any jury.

The Fashion-Conscious Neanderthal

Beads have existed for at least 40,000 years—possibly 100,000 or more. Heck, they're almost as old as Dick Clark! Some early examples of beads, composed of grooved teeth and bones, were discovered in France, thus demonstrating that the French have *always* been fashion forward. In ensuing eons, beads took prehistoric civilization by storm, sweeping beyond the borders of Europe to such diverse regions as Australia, Asia, Africa, and the Americas, each wee ornament reflecting its wearer's social circumstances and knack for accessorizing.

As human-ish types matured from hunting and gathering to farming and settling, they discovered that not having to travel so much for work meant they had more time for hobbies, like beading. Moreover, this new-and-improved societal model allowed these knuckle-draggers to turn their attention from such mundane matters as outwitting carnivores in order to survive to a far more critical issue: fashion.

Suddenly, using teeth and bones as beads was *so* last era, not to mention sort of creepy. Everyone who was anyone started wearing jewelry composed of shells and semi-precious stones such as carnelian, lapis lazuli, agate, turquoise, serpentine, and amber.

Glass Warfare

Look, no one's saying that the beads worn by early hominids weren't pretty and all. It's just that, well, not everyone could afford them. Enter the Harappan Civilization in the Indus Valley (that's Pakistan and western India to you and me) and the Egyptians. Independently from each other, these crafty folks developed and mass-produced a material called *faience* circa 4000 BC. Craftsmen used this finely glazed, quartz-based ceramic material, now seen as a forerunner to glass, to simulate precious stones such as turquoise and lapis. Even better fakes became available with the advent of actual glass some 1,700 years later; by 1350 BC, the glassmaking process having been perfected, even the humblest of folk boasted a bit of bling.

Upon Egypt's decline, which coincided with the fall of the New Kingdom in 1085 BC, the seafaring Phoenicians—who had long traded Egypt's beads abroad—cut out the middleman by leaping into the glassmaking fray themselves. They are credited with discovering a technique that yielded transparent, rather than opaque, glass, a development that eyeglass wearers of today particularly appreciate. When Phoenicia went the way of Egypt, Rome became the flat world's glassmaking hub. Indeed, thanks to advances in techniques and technology, outposts of the Roman Empire—namely, the areas now known as Syria, Egypt, Italy, Switzerland, the Rhineland, France, and England—produced more glass beads in the first century AD than had been turned out in all previous 500 years.

The Roman Empire might have won the glassmaking games in the short term, but India, which began manufacturing fake gemstones from glass as early as the fourth century BC, proved victorious over the long haul. One port town, Arikamedu, enjoyed nearly uninterrupted bead production until the 1600s AD. And these beads weren't sold just locally; by the first century AD, beads manufactured in India had migrated as far as Taiwan, Indonesia, and the Philippines.

Unfortunately, like many good things—baths come to mind—beading in Europe fell out of favor among the rank and file citizenry after the fall of Rome in AD 476 (although archaeological evidence does suggest that beading remained a cottage industry during the Middle Ages). No doubt, this decline was in part because the Catholic Church deemed it impious—nay, *flamboyant*—to wear beads, although beads, in the form of rosaries, were permitted for prayer and meditation.

Interestingly, even as Catholic leaders snubbed beads, followers of Islam, who inhabited the desert lands that envelop the Red Sea, heartily embraced them. Indeed, the Koran describes stars as "beads of the sky." Between AD 700 and AD 1400, Muslims wore strands of prayer beads, and also wore beads to convey their social status. Islamic beads from this period bear distinctive decorations resulting from such techniques as trailing, feathering, dragging, and folding. Unfortunately, the AD 1401 invasion of the Mongols, coupled with the fall of Constantinople in 1453, put the kibosh on the creation of these Islamic beads.

Venice II Society

Eventually, Catholic Church officials, supported by the aristocracy, decided flamboyance wasn't so bad after all—which may at least partially explain how it came to pass that glassmaking was revived in Europe circa AD 1200, in Venice. A more powerful driver, however, was the dramatic increase in merchant trade. Simply put, small and shiny as they were, beads made great currency—exchangeable for such goodies as silk, porcelain, spices, ivory, and pelts. (Beads were also traded for slaves, but because that is evil and depressing, I shan't discuss it further.)

The Venetians weren't messing around. Master craftsmen and their assistants put in 12-hour shifts, day and night, dousing their furnaces only for repairs and holidays. Through experimentation, Venetian glassmakers hit upon just the right formula of silica, salts, lime, and other minerals to make glass of varying types and colors, as well as a technique to strengthen it. To protect Venice proper from the fire hazards posed by their furnaces, and to ensure that their trade secrets remained safe, Venetian glassmakers relocated their factories across the bog to the island of Murano. Vigilante-style governance by the Committee of Ten, charged with policing the glassmakers, further protected the trade; thanks to them, anyone who revealed glassmaking secrets to outsiders got whacked.

Although some Venetian glassmakers specialized in plates, others in vases, yada yada yada, beads were the cash crop. The colorful millefiori and chevron beads were especially prized. By 1606, the greater Venice metropolitan area boasted more than 250 bead producers. Throughout the 17th and 18th centuries, these craftsmen churned out between 175,000 and 280,000 pounds of beads each year—comparable to *seven* Kirstie Alleys (pre–Jenny Craig)— all bound for locales near and far. Eager to get their piece of the pie, bead-making enterprises ramped up across Europe, most notably in Bohemia and the Netherlands.

A Snitch in Time

Because the Committee of Ten has long since dissolved, I feel I can safely inform you that Venetian glassmakers typically manufactured beads using one of two techniques: the wound lampwork technique; or the drawn method. Wound lampwork involved torching glass cane–sticks of glass that look like those old-fashioned candy sticks that were really pretty but didn't always taste all that great–until it went molten, and then wrapping the molten glass around a metal rod to form a shape. Several layers of glass in varying colors were often used, all to create one single freaking bead. The more efficient–albeit less artful–technique was the drawn method, which involved blowing molten glass into a bubble, attaching metal plates to the bubble, and then pulling in opposite directions to create a hollow cane. (Amazingly, skilled glassmakers could create canes upward of 300 feet long–that's a football field to you and me.) Once the cane hardened, it could then be sliced and diced into a gazillion little beads.

An example of a millefiori bead.
        Chevron beads like this one were also prized.

Out of Africa

Well before European traders docked in Africa, even before the arrival of the Phoenicians and then the Arabs, African cultures engaged in their own form of bead making. Archaeologists estimate that the earliest known examples of African beads—disk-shaped and composed of ostrich eggshells—date back some 12,000 years. By the fourth century AD, glass beads, generally considered the most common feature of traditional African adornment, had found their way to the continent. When the Portuguese arrived in the 15th and 16th centuries, and the Dutch, British, French, Belgians, and Germans thereafter, they continued to supply beads to an existing market. And a thriving market it was—some African kings donned beaded regalia that was so heavy, they needed helpers to support them when moving about. Sort of like Liberace.

Code Breaker

For members of many African tribes, beads were—and, in many cases, remain—more than just ornaments or status symbols. They were, you might say, among the earliest forms of instant messaging. Take the Zulus of South Africa. The types and colors of beads they wore, the patterns and shapes in which those beads were presented, and the background upon which they appeared conveyed to others the wearer's marital or dating status, an emotion the wearer was feeling, details of a past event, even love letters. Just to confuse things, the use of certain colors meant that the *opposite* of what you read in the pattern was true—think passive-aggressive beading.

East of Beadin'

The far east—namely, China, Korea, and Japan—had its own beading tradition, distinct and independent from the one that developed in the west. The oldest beads found in the region, which were made from the bones of deer toes and unearthed in a cave in Turobong, Korea, date back 20,000 years. Early examples of Chinese beads, dated at 16,000 BC, are made from stone, with subsequent styles using ostrich eggshells and even fossilized dinosaur eggshells. Later, Chinese societies prized jade beads, which entered the scene around 1500 BC; indeed, the Chinese written character for "bead" is identical to the character for "jade" (as are the characters in Korean and Japanese). Thanks to the Silk Road routes, China, Korea, and Japan enjoyed a steady supply of this material—along with coral, lapis, glass, turquoise, and amber— over a 1,200 year period beginning in 200 BC. Glass, too, became a favored bead ingredient; during a 300-year period beginning in the fourth century BC, the Chinese created their own glass beads, called "eye beads," which are still regarded as among the loveliest beads ever fabricated. Not to be overlooked are the peoples of Southeast Asia, who, at least as early as 2500 BC, used beads for such diverse purposes as personal adornment, protection, status symbols, sacred altar objects, even dowries.

New World Beader

Okay, so the European explorers made it a habit to decimate the native populations of the New World either by force or by flu. Case in point: during the period between 1519 and 1533, a measly 24 years, Spanish conquistadors effectively destroyed both the Aztec and the Inca civilizations. I'll give you that. But at least they tried to soften the blow for these doomed people by doling out some Venetian glass beads along the way. I mean, they weren't *totally* insensitive.

Unfortunately, I'm guessing the beads, pretty though they may have been, offered little consolation, especially to the civilizations that called modern-day South and Central America home; after all, it wasn't like these indigenous people had never seen a bead before. Snail-shell beads unearthed in southern Mexico date back nearly 10,000 years. And the Aztecs produced a variety of gorgeous beads, the most prized of them made of jade and gold, for adornment and ceremonial purposes. Likewise, the tribes that roamed North America had their own beading traditions, having worn and traded beads composed of shell, pearl, bone, teeth, stone, and fossils some 8,000 years before Columbus plowed his *Niña*, *Pinta*, and *Santa Maria* into theretofore unblemished shores. Later, artisans crafted beads from such materials as gold, jade, and turquoise. (Actually, if you want to get all technical about it, glass beads were actually introduced to native North Americans by the Vikings, but they didn't really take root. It wasn't until Columbus's arrival in 1492 that Native Americans embraced the glass bead.)

You're So Money, Baby

The Native Americans along the Eastern seaboard didn't just wear beads; they sometimes used them as cash. Specifically, they used beads made from shells as currency—usually white shells, but sometimes the more rare (and hence more desirable) purple. The Narragansett tribe called these beads *wampumpeag*, for "white shell beads." European settlers, who couldn't waste precious time pronouncing *wampumpeag*, shortened it to *wampum*.

Because the beads used as wampum were difficult to make, it made for stable currency; indeed, due to shortages in coin money, even the white settlers used wampum as legal tender for a time, both with the native population and among themselves. In fact, students at Harvard, established in 1636, could pay their tuition in wampum. And as white settlers shoved further and further into the interior, they used wampum to buy land, furs, and services.

Eventually, however, the settlers figured out how to mass-produce passable facsimiles of both the white and the purple varieties of wampum, sometimes using other, more abundant materials. By the 1700s, Dutch factories manufactured vast quantities of faux wampum. Thus, the factors that had long kept the wampum economy stable—the time-intensive practice of creating beads from shells and the rarity of the purple shells in particular—were removed. Because settlers could produce wampum at a comparatively blistering rate, the wampum-based economy destabilized, and wampum itself became devalued.

The mass production of wampum disrupted the wampum-based economy, which was bad. On the plus side, the glut of wampum allowed Native Americans to divert the shells used to create it to more artful purposes—namely, belts, bracelets, necklaces, and collars. The belts, in particular, served a dual purpose: 1) to minimize figure flaws, obviously, and 2) to conduct diplomatic

Manhattan Transfer

If you're like me, you were told by well-meaning teachers that Dutch settlers bought Manhattan with a string of beads. As compelling as this story might be—especially to someone like me, who could realistically be suckered into just such a real-estate transaction, especially if the beads were rully rully sparkly—it's short on what Stephen Colbert calls "truthiness." Recent scholarship indicates that there is no evidence to support the notion that beads were part of the deal.

relations with other tribes. As to the latter, Native Americans wove wampum into designs that communicated declarations of war, offers of peace, or invitations to the next social mixer.

We Got Spirits, Yes We Do!

It wasn't just that beads were pretty, although, of course, they *totally* are. And it wasn't just that they could be used as currency or to communicate with others. Beads have also served a spiritual purpose since the Flintstone era. Our early forebears believed that beads gave hunters an edge over their prey, brought good luck, and could protect them from harm. In fact, the English word "bead" derives from the Anglo-Saxon "bede," meaning "prayer." As modern organized religions took root, beads became instrumental in prayer; if, like two-thirds of the world's population, you call yourself Buddhist, Hindu, Muslim, or Christian, you likely employ prayer beads when asking your deity for health, happiness, or prosperity, or for the Chicago Cubs to finally win a freaking pennant.

Lighten Up, It's Just Fashion

As anyone who watches *Project Runway* can tell you, the fashion cycle involves six distinct phases: innovation, rise, acceleration, general acceptance, decline, and obsolescence. During, say, the Upper Paleolithic, the fashion cycle lasted eons. Literally. As civilizations developed and later intertwined through trade, this cycle contracted, but remained hostage to the inherently slow schedule of the hand-craftsman. The Industrial Revolution, however, which occurred in England between 1750 and 1830, put fashion cycles—including those related to jewelry—in hyper drive. Where the creation of jewelry, beaded bags, and the like formerly required the patience, skill, and care of a craftsman, a machine could now do the job in nothing flat. Moreover, the Industrial Revolution also yielded the machinery necessary to automate some aspects of mining, which led to an avalanche of available gemstones. As a result, the burgeoning middle class enjoyed a new-found ability to wear jewelry that went beyond the simple strand of glass beads; indeed, they could wear pieces that looked quite like those belonging to their betters. It's no surprise, then, that to some degree, beads, especially of the glass variety, fell out of favor.

And the Bead Goes On...

Of course, the fashion cycle wasn't dictated only by advancements in the field of manufacturing. The tide of world events also determined the rise and fall of fashion trends. Here are but a few examples:

♦ When British Queen Victoria's beloved husband, Albert, succumbed to typhoid fever in 1861, Victoria entered a period of mourning—*for 40 freaking years.* As the queen's personal style shifted to a palette that Spïnal Tap's Nigel Tufnel would undoubtedly describe as "none more black," so, too, did the entire nation's.

The Agony of Effete

Not everyone embraced the changes wrought by the Industrial Revolution. Just as rich people today will gladly spend $197 for a hand-painted T-shirt in SoHo but would rather be caught dead than wear a $4.92 Wal-Mart knock-off, the cultural elite of the day viewed mass-produced items with some degree of disdain. It wasn't just that the uniformity of these objects screamed soullessness (which, of course, they did); mainly, it was the simple fact that working types could afford goodies like mass-produced jewelry that made that jewelry anathema to the upper crust. This attitude gave rise to several anti-bling movements, most notably the Aesthetes, who eschewed ostentation on all fronts, as well as the Arts and Crafts movement, also called the Liberty Style, led by John Ruskin and William Morris, which focused on hand-crafted pieces. England's Arts and Crafts movement was closely associated with other movements across the globe: Art Nouveau in France's café society, Jugendstil in Germany, Modernismo in Spain, Secessionstil in Austria, and Stile Liberty in Italy. Indeed, the sensibilities of the Arts and Crafts movement even spread as far as Russia, as evidenced by the magnificent designs of Carl Fabergé, and the United States, where Tiffany's led the charge. Characterized by florid, fanciful motifs that celebrated the mysteries of nature and the sensuality of the female form, the style horrified the mainstream of the day—which, I suspect, was precisely the point.

♦ The drab fare of Victoria's day fell out of favor when Victoria's son Edward assumed the throne after her death in 1901. British fashion whiplashed back to a more lively style—one that reflected the nation's prosperity, status, and confidence.

♦ The *Titanic,* en route from Southampton to New York, nullified claims of its unsinkability by plowing into a North Atlantic iceberg in 1912, thereby killing Leonardo DiCaprio and 1,499 other passengers. As if that wasn't enough of a buzzkill, some Serbian nut job triggered World War I 2 years later by offing Franz Ferdinand (the archduke of Austro-Hungary, not the band) and his wife as they paraded through Sarajevo. Ensuing years saw some nine million souls extinguished by the war; the onset of the Russian Revolution in 1917; a global influenza epidemic in 1918; and Prohibition in America in 1919. Not surprisingly, fashion turned glum once again, favoring drab palettes.

♦ The 1920s brought a respite from the grim realities of war—at least for the victors. Scrimping and saving was *so* last decade; frivolity was the order of the day. Fashion became less formal, less restrictive. Women, who had enjoyed their first taste of freedom while their men were at war, ditched their corsets, bobbed their hair, powdered their noses, and showed a bit of leg. Indeed, hemlines rose scandalously high during this period, stopping just above the knee. This era also witnessed the resurgence of beads—in particular, to embellish garments, and for costume jewelry. The predominant style was Art Deco, which featured a wide range of motifs and drew from such disparate influences as Egyptian, African, Asian, and Native American art.

- The stock market crash of 1929, which ushered in the Great Depression, put the kibosh on the fun of the Roaring 20s. As the economies of the United States and Europe collapsed, the most sought-after accessory was the calorie.

- The advent of yet another world war, largely the result of Adolph Hitler's successful marketing of a new and improved brand of evil, drove the urge to adorn yet further underground. Nonetheless, although many of the materials formerly used to manufacture jewelry were requisitioned for the war effort, designers used whatever they had in stock to create new pieces that not only pleased the eye but also commented on world events. A prime example was the House of Cartier's Bird in the Cage and Freed Bird lines, meant as a slam on France's pro-Nazi Vichy regime.

- Victory by the Allies swung the pendulum of fashion away from the necessarily austere look of the war years to a lusher, more feminine sensibility. Fashion designer Christian Dior launched his "New Look," characterized by longer lengths and fuller skirts. Likewise, jewelers designed fresh, pretty baubles to reflect the peace.

- In the late 1960s, beads made a triumphant comeback, with handmade beaded necklaces—called *love beads*—symbolizing brotherly love and acceptance, catch words of the Civil Rights era. If you were looking to piss off your parents, love beads—plus, of course, flea-infested hair, bell-bottoms, a tie-dyed shirt, and an ample supply of mind-altering drugs—were the way to go.

- Fashion swung the opposite direction in the 1980s. The sloppy styles of the late 1960s and 1970s gave way to a "greed is good" sensibility, one that was equal parts *Dynasty*, *Dallas*, *Wall Street*, and Dame Edna Everage.

- In retaliation of the excesses of the 1980s, the 1990s brought *grunge*, characterized by flannel shirts, dirty jeans, Doc Martens, and greasy hair; a punk revival followed close on its heels. Jewelry styles tended toward the industrial.

- In the years since 2000, we've seen jewelry styles ranging from chokers to pearls with ribbons for clasps to granny brooches to Liberace-size cocktail rings to chandelier earrings to . . . pretty much *anything*.

All right, look. Here's my point: If the fashion cycle is going to continue to change every 7 seconds (and there's little to indicate that it won't), and if you're going to keep apace (which, genetically speaking, seems to go without saying), you're either going to need to win the lottery or learn how to make some pieces for yourself (preferably both). And that, *mes amies*, is where I come in. In this book, I'll show you how to break the beading code to make your own dazzling pieces. As for the lottery, you're on your own.

Next!

In the next chapter, you'll find out the most critical part of any undertaking: what you get to buy.

Chapter Two

◆◆◆

The Good Buy Girl

H ere it is, the best part of any new endeavor: finding out what you get to buy. In this chapter you'll discover the materials and tools required of any new beader, as well as explore the various types of beads available. If you're ready to feed your need to bead, read on!

We Got the Bead: Types of Beads

Remember that *Sex and the City* episode where Carrie realizes she's squandered more than $40,000 on shoes? I had a similarly revelatory experience when I tallied up the amount of money I've frittered on beads. Here's the problem: There are *so many* types of beads, plus they are often rully rully shiny. To enable you to whittle down your own savings, I've provided you with a rundown of some of the more popular and beautiful bead varieties:

- ◆ **Crystal beads.** Austria. It's not just the setting for *The Sound of Music*; it's also where Swarovski crystals, the undisputed champ in the crystal-bead division, are made. If your objective is to blind your companions, this is the bead for you. Prized for their shine, these sparklers are available in an array of colors.

- ◆ **Lampwork beads.** These handmade glass wonders are the Volkswagen Bug of beads—they are colorful, are cheerful, often feature flowers, and are usually round-ish.

Lampwork beads

Polymer beads

♦ **Metal beads.** These include base metal beads (i.e., aluminum, brass, bronze, copper, and nickel), gold-filled beads, silver- and 18-karat-gold-plated beads, sterling silver beads, and vermeil (a.k.a. sterling silver electroplated with gold). Not to be overlooked, charms, which are usually made of metal, can also be used in your beadwork.

♦ **Polymer beads.** Polymers aren't just for NASA anymore! These days, artisans frequently use a claylike polymer—think FiMo and Sculpey—to hand-craft lightweight, colorful, interesting beads.

Dr. Feelgood

If you're looking for a cure for crabbiness (or, say, crabs), you'll be happy to learn that some people think certain semi-precious stones and other materials possess healing properties.

♦ **Agate** is believed to improve vitality, increase self-confidence, balance emotions, calm the body, reduce fever, banish fear, improve eloquence, and, for the dentally challenged, harden tender gums.

♦ **Amethyst** is said to counter addiction, relieve stress, protect against acne, and—write this one down—offset drunkenness. In case you forget to wear an amethyst the next time you bar-hop, invest in **atacamite,** which can be used to treat certain venereal diseases, and in **peridot,** which both treats bruised eyes and helps mend damaged relationships.

♦ **Aquamarine** supposedly preserves innocence and increases self-knowledge (unless, presumably, your innocence is sullied by some very painful, hard truths about yourself).

♦ **Beryl** guards against stupidity. *Your* stupidity, that is. Not, sadly, the stupidity of those around you.

- **Precious and semi-precious beads.** If you are not a Rockefeller and you've never won the lottery, you face a dilemma: Do you plunder your emergency fund to buy beads made of precious stones, such as rubies and emeralds, for your higher-end beading projects? Or do you settle for semi-precious beads such as amethyst, aquamarine, garnet, jade, onyx, peridot, quartz, and topaz? Do you opt for pricey sea-crafted pearls or their cheaper freshwater counterparts? You decide.

- **Pressed glass beads.** These are your run-of-the-mill glass beads, available in an array of sizes and colors. Shapes can range from plain round to flowers, puppies, rocket ships, and beyond.

- **Resin beads.** These sturdy, durable beads typically boast the color and opacity of popsicles.

- **Seed beads.** A variety of beading techniques, especially those involving stitching or weaving, employ seed beads. These are small, mass-produced beads that look a lot like teeny, tiny, er, seeds. You can purchase seed beads in a variety of sizes from practically microscopic (i.e., size 24) to somewhat itty-bitty (i.e., sizes 4, 5, or 6). Seed beads, which are usually glass, are also sold in an array of shapes including rocaille (these are round-ish), charlotte (these have facets), and bugle (these are, like, totally tubular). Seed beads are also categorized according to where they're made, with Czech seed beads being the most common and Japanese seed beads, called *delicas*, ranking a close second.

- **Wood beads.** Often manufactured in Germany, wood beads can be found in a multitude of colors, shapes, and sizes. If you plan to sell your pieces out of the hatchback of your rusted-out Saab while tailing the next Grateful Dead/Phish/Widespread Panic–type band, wood is the material for you. That's not to say, however, that there aren't some pretty kickin' wood beads suitable for a slightly more modern aesthetic.

Assuage Your Social Conscience

Not to be all buzzkill about things, but if you're if you're a card-carrying member of PETA–or if you're afraid of being accosted by one–then you'll want to avoid using bone and horn beads in your beadwork. Although these types of beads, which are usually hand-carved in Indonesia and the Philippines, do make lovely adornments, you just can't overlook the fact that there's a good chance the animal from whence said bone and/or horn came probably would have preferred to keep those bits in their original skeletal form. Moreover, buying certain types of bone and horn–ivory comes to mind–is actually illegal except when it's antique. Unless you look especially good in bright orange jumpsuits and shackles, stick to using other materials.

Beauty Comes in All Shapes and Sizes

Within each variety of bead, further choices emerge thanks to differences in size and shape. Self-explanatory shapes include round, tube, cube, oval, drop, barrel, bicone, and button. Then there are what I call the "food-group" shapes: potato, rice, melon, wafer, chip, chiclet, and donut. (Mmm. Donut. Doh! Now I'm hungry.)

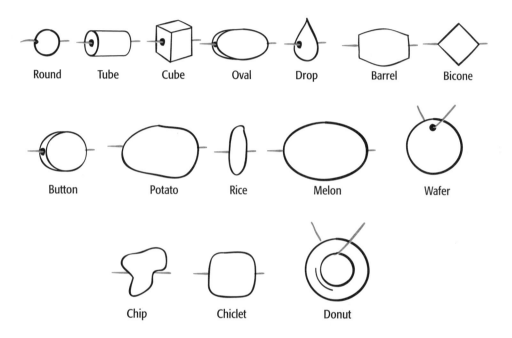

Round, tube, cube, oval, drop, barrel, bicone, button, potato, rice, melon, wafer, chip, chiclet, and donut shaped beads.

Beyond that, you'll likely encounter the following bead shapes:

- **Keishi.** Not to be confused with Kashi (which, I might add, is very tasty and chock-full of fiber), Keishi beads are shaped like Keishi pearls. Considered accidents of a pearl's culturing process—the "Elephant Man of the sea," if you will—Keishi pearls are perhaps best described as "blobby."

- **Heishi.** Literally translated "shell," *heishi* refers to tiny, uniform, cylindrical beads crafted from shells. Better strands of heishi—pronounced "he-she" (think "transvestite")—resemble liquid, snakelike cylinders. These days, heishi-style beads are made not just from shells but also from coral, turquoise, jet, and even plastic.

- **Rondelle.** The Rondelles, in addition to being a New Wave girl group from Washington, D.C., circa 1998–2001—famous for such audio gems as "Fake Fight," "Drag Strip Race," and "Cafeteria Rock" ("I wanna BEAN BURRITO, EXTRA JALAPEÑO!")—are also Frisbee-shaped beads. Rondelles are similar to buttons but are drilled *through* the flat portion rather than across it, making them great spacer beads.

Keishi beads Heishi beads Rondelle beads

Materials Girl

Of course, mere beads do not a bauble make. Before you embark on any beading project, you'll need to stock up on some other materials. Depending on the type of piece you plan to assemble—necklace, earrings, scale beaded-wire replica of Liberace's rhinestone-encrusted Superpiano—these additional supplies may include the following:

- Thread and/or wire
- Needles
- Findings
- Glue

Right Said Thread

A visit to any beading store will reveal a pu-pu platter of thread, cord, ribbon, chain, and wire. Plus, you'll need to select thread color that won't clash with your beads. It's enough to turn even the most decisive girl into a ditherer. Here's the lowdown:

- **Nylon thread.** This thread, which is sold in various widths and colors, works well for woven bead projects or for stitching beads onto, say, a dog collar or Narciso Rodriguez gown. Words to the wise: Don't use nylon thread if your project involves large, heavy beads; opt for stronger string.

Wax On

Seasoned beaders coat their nylon thread with wax to prevent fraying and knotting. Beeswax is a common choice; it can be purchased in bar form or in nuggets shaped tantalizingly like Reese's Peanut Butter Cups. Alternatives to beeswax include synthetic, petroleum-based beeswax (a.k.a. *microcrystalline wax* for you science-y types) and Thread Heaven, which is a wax-ish thread conditioner that enables you to both smooth the thread and magnetize it with static electricity to help reduce pesky knots. The drill is generally to grasp one end of your thread (after it's been cut) and slide it back and forth across the wax or conditioner until the thread is coated.

- **Silk thread.** Silk thread, a gorgeous, natural material available in a cornucopia of colors and thicknesses, knots easily, making it ideal for stringing your more delicate (read: girly and expensive) beads. Be aware, however, that silk can fray, and that cosmetics and oil on your skin (no offense) can weaken silk.

- **FireLine.** This braided thread is made of a NASA-sounding material called "gel-spun polyetholine." It's very strong and knots easily.

- **Elastic thread.** If you have the attention span of cotton, then elastic thread is the stringing material for you. Why? Because it enables you to crank out a bracelet in less time than it takes to climb the six flights of stairs to your studio walkup. Just string your beads, knot the elastic, *et voilá.*

- **Monofilament.** If you've ever gone fishing to impress an outdoorsy boy, you may already be familiar with monofilament thread; it is commonly used for angling. In addition to enabling you to hook a 15-pound sturgeon, monofilament thread can also be used to knot a lovely necklace. If you like card tricks and sleight of hand, you'll especially appreciate this stringing material. Also called *illusion cord,* monofilament, which is usually clear in color, enables you to create jewelry pieces whose beads appear to be suspended in thin air. (Beat that, David Copperfield!) As a bonus, it's easy on the pocketbook.

- **Fiber cord.** In addition to smoking hemp (for medical reasons, of course), you can also use hemp—as well as linen and jute—to knit and crochet beads, fashion hippie-ish bracelets, and macramé lovely—if somewhat dated—plant hangers.

- **Leather cord.** Perfect for jewelry featuring large, wide-holed beads, leather cord, which is generally smooth in texture, can be found in a variety of colors.

- **Suede cord.** See "Leather cord," but ignore the "smooth in texture" part.

- **Satin cord.** Satin cord, which is slippery like satin sheets, is categorized into three widths: rattail, mousetail, and bugtail, with rattail being the thickest and bugtail the thinnest. If you can get past the rodent- and pest-based terminology, then you'll find satin cord to be a great option, especially if you're working with large beads.

- **Ribbon.** Remember that ghost story about the guy who marries a lady who always wears a blue ribbon tied around her neck? Over and over, she cautions him, usually in a very spooky voice, "Don't untie the ribbon!" Being a man, he either doesn't hear her or simply can't follow directions, and he unties the ribbon anyway—only to recoil in horror when her head falls off. Although no ribbon currently on the market will enable you to join your noggin with your neck in the event you are decapitated, several can be used to make a smashing necklace or bracelet.

- **Chain.** If you're Ali G., Eminem, or otherwise livin' gangsta style, and you're looking for just the right string for your bling, chain is a great option. It's also nice for charm bracelets.

- **Beading wire.** Technically speaking, beading wire is, well, wire, but it acts like thread. For one, it is available in a range of widths. And unlike other types of wire, beading wire is supple and flexible, and some varieties of beading wire can even be knotted. Beading wire is composed of multiple strands of steel coated with nylon; hence, you'll want to use wire cutters in lieu of, say, your teeth to cut it.

- **Tiger tail.** Like beading wire, tiger tail is technically wire but acts more like thread. In the interest of unbiased reporting, however, I should disclose that you can't really knot tiger tail, and God help you if you put a kink in it.

- **Memory wire.** Like elastic, memory wire is ideal for short–attention-span beaders. Made of tempered stainless steel and sold in a variety of gauges, memory wire comes pre-coiled in ring, bracelet, and necklace form. Be aware that if you use memory wire, you'll want to purchase special memory-wire cutters to cut it—either that or offer up your good wire cutters to the beading gods.

- **Base metal wire.** Brass, copper, and steel wire can be purchased on the cheap in a variety of gauges, and is great for practicing wirework beading techniques. Copper wire tends to be the most flexible of the bunch, and steel wire the most rigid. If you're going for a ritzier look but are already a month behind on your rent, use copper or brass wire coated with a thin layer of 14-karat gold and pretend it's solid.

- **Sterling silver wire.** Thanks to sterling silver wire's versatility, jewelry makers have voted this material "Most Popular." Composed of 92.5 percent silver and 7.5 percent copper, this medium is offered in a variety of gauges. It's also sold in a variety of hard-nesses, with dead soft being most like the filters used to film Cybil Shepherd in *Moonlighting:* soft and forgiving. If your aim is to sell your pieces, using sterling silver wire in lieu of, say, base metal wire will enable you to charge way more—putting you square in the running for "Most Likely to Succeed."

- **Niobium wire.** Strong and hypoallergenic, niobium is the Mr. Sensitive Ponytail of wire. In addition, it's sold in a variety of colors—pink, purple, dark blue, teal, green, and gold. If you're sick of silver, niobium wire is for you.

Smooth Operator

If the holes drilled in your beads are a bit rough around the edges, or if they're a hair too small to accommodate your thread of choice, consider keeping a round file and a bead reamer handy. Round files look a bit like incense sticks; you poke them into your bead, twist it back and forth a few times, and withdraw it, the result being smoother innards for your bead. Bead reamers look a bit like picks for very very small ice cubes; you poke the sharp end of the reamer into your bead and work it around a few times to enlarge the hole. (Of course, you're a bit limited in how much you can enlarge a bead's hole without destroying the bead altogether. If you're dealing with particularly delicate beads, you might just be S.O.L. if your thread is too thick. If so, just suck it up and use a different type of thread.)

So how do you decide what stringing material to use with the beads you've selected? First, take a hard look at your beads. Do they have smooth drill holes? If so, you can use any stringing material your little heart desires, provided it's strong enough to hold your beads and thin enough to fit through said drill holes. If your beads are a bit rough around the edges, or are particularly heavy, then you might want to limit yourself to beading wire, braided thread, fiber cord, leather cord, satin cord, or suede cord.

Needles to Say

Like hard drugs, not all beading projects require the use of a needle. If you're hoping to complete any projects that involve stitching, however, you'll want some on hand. Don't assume, though, that the needle that came with the sewing kit you filched from your hotel room in Las Vegas will do the trick. Although run-of-the-mill sewing needles will suffice for some pieces, others require actual beading needles. In particular, you'll want to keep the following types of needles around:

- **Beading needles.** Bead suppliers sell these needles in a range of lengths and sizes—#10, #12, #13, #15, and #16 (the smallest). The distinguishing characteristic of a beading needle is that its eye is the same width as the rest of the needle, which is itself very fine. This feature is particularly handy if your project involves beads with minuscule holes.

- **Sharps.** Sharps are beading needles that are noted for their, er, sharpness. They're also very sturdy, and are shorter than regular beading needles. If your project involves a peyote stitch, a sharp is the way to go—unless you're also smoking peyote, in which case I suggest you avoid needles altogether.

- **Big eye needles.** These wire needles are 90 percent eye, 10 percent point, making them by far the easiest to thread. Just separate the center wires and poke the tip of the thread through. If your project simply involves stringing rather than stitching or weaving, a big eye needle can easily do the job.

♦ **Twisted wire needles.** These flexible, blunt needles, characterized by a large loop on one end and a twisted shank on the other, work best with small-holed beads; as the needle passes through the bead's hole, the loop collapses.

Beading needles   Big eye needles   Twisted wire needles

Once you have the needle threaded, your instinct will likely be to hold the needle with one hand and use your fingertips on the other hand to pinch beads from your work surface—preferably a felt bead mat, which you can buy at any bead store, so the beads don't all roll onto the floor—and then carefully place them onto the tip of the needle. Resist. The preferred (read: quicker) method is to use the needle's tip to "pick" beads from your mat. Simply poke the tip of your needle through the hole of a bead that's lying on your mat and flick your wrist such that the bead slides down the shaft of the needle unassisted. Repeat until no more beads will fit on the shaft, and then slide all the beads down the shaft onto your thread. You'll be glad you mastered this technique the next time you put off stringing seven necklaces for your best friend's bridal party until the night of the rehearsal dinner.

Findings Keepers

The term *findings* refers to the wee bits of hardware used to create beaded (and other) jewelry. A sure-fire way to cheapen your pieces is to use sub-par findings. Use the best findings you can afford—especially if you plan to sell your jewelry or give it to people who you want to like you. These findings include but are not limited to the following:

- ♦ **Rings.** In this context, *ring* refers to a small circle of wire used to connect bits of bead-work. Beading involves two main types of rings: jump rings and split rings. A *jump ring* is simply a single ring of wire that features a small opening, which you open and close by bending the wire sideways (rather than apart and together). Split rings, in contrast, are like Lilliputian key rings. In general, split rings are more secure than jump rings because they are more difficult to pry apart. If split rings become your ring of choice, invest in a pair of split ring

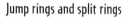

Jump rings and split rings

pliers. They make the task of opening the split rings easy enough that you won't need to be committed to a mental institution afterward. I talk more about split ring pliers a little later on.

- ♦ **Pins.** Keeping an array of pins handy is a smart move. Eye pins and head pins, which have blunt rather than the pointy tips of their sewing pin counterparts, are often used to create dangly earrings. Head pins typically resemble anorexic nails—that is, they are composed of a skinny strand of wire with a flat stopper on one end. Eye pins resemble head pins except they use a loop as the stopper. Ball pins are also common—they're just like head pins but have a little ball on the end rather than a nail head. Pins also come in more embellished forms, with pretty designs acting as stoppers. As an aside, straight pins,

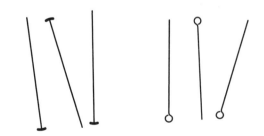

Head pins and eye pins

corsage pins (sorry, minus the corsage), and their ilk can come in handy when you begin stringing jewelry.

- ♦ **Ear wires.** If dangly earrings are your game, you'll need to invest in ear wires. French ear wires—excuse me, make that *freedom* ear wires—look like upside-down Js with a loop on one end, which you open as you would a jump ring to hang your dangly bits. Kidney wires, on the other hand, resemble, er, kidneys. In addition to French and

Dangly earrings that use French ear wires can slip out of your earlobe, which is a huge bummer if the earring featured super special (read: expensive) beads. To prevent such catastrophes, invest in some plastic stoppers, like the ones frequently found on store-bought earrings. They're typically sold separately from the ear wires themselves, but can generally be found on the cheap at any bead store and at most craft stores.

kidney wires, you can also use lever backs. These look like kidney wires but are closed with a lever, making them more secure. (Of course, in addition to using ear wires to create earrings, you can also employ hoops, clip-ons, and posts.)

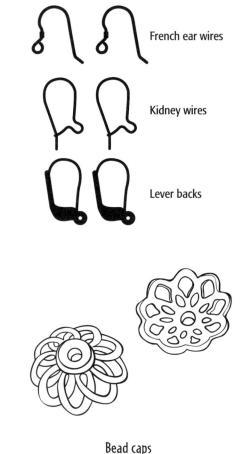

French ear wires

Kidney wires

Lever backs

♦ **Bead caps.** Sometimes called "cup beads," these are used to cover roughness or damage near the drilled portion of a bead, as well as to embellish your piece. They aren't required, but can add that special sump'm-sump'm.

♦ **Clamshells.** These doo-dads, also called calottes (not to be confused with *culottes*, which are unflattering shorts-ish/pants-ish/skirt-ish garments), can be used (but are not required) to attach a clasp to the body of your piece. Bead tips perform a similar function.

♦ **Cones.** If you're constructing a multi-strand piece, you might want to employ a cone to conceal the portion of the piece where the strands come together.

Bead caps

♦ **Crimp beads.** Tube-shaped, metal, and teeny, crimp beads can be used to attach a clasp to your strung piece. Simply string the crimp bead onto your thread, poke the thread through your clasp, and then pull the thread in the opposite direction back through the crimp bead. Then—this is the fun part, where you can work out

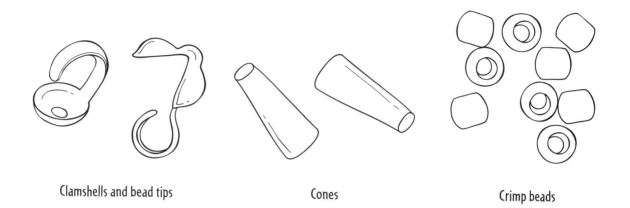

Clamshells and bead tips   Cones   Crimp beads

some aggression—squish the bead flat using crimping pliers. (Note that in addition to crimp beads, you'll also run across crimp bands that are built into clasps, typically used to attach leather cord to the clasp. You squish these bands with chain nose pliers rather than crimping pliers.)

♦ **Connectors, separator bars, and end bars.** If you're planning a piece with multiple strands, you might consider incorporating connectors, separator bars, and/or end bars. Connectors are helpful if you want your piece to start with a single strand and then switch to multiple stands partway through. Separator bars, also called spacer bars, tidy up multiple-strand pieces by separating and spacing the strands. End bars enable you to join multiple strands to a single-strand clasp.

♦ **Clasps.** Clasps, also called fasteners, open and close, enabling you to, say, fasten a necklace around your neck. Clasps are sold in many flavors; my faves are lobster-claw, toggle, and S-hook. In addition to serving a functional purpose, clasps can also beautify your piece—especially clasps with decorative embellishments or gemstones.

Connectors, separator bars,
and end bars

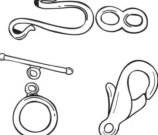

Lobster-claw clasp, toggle clasp,
and S-hook clasp

Stick with Me, Kid: Glues and Adhesives

Remember when John Malkovich appeared on *Saturday Night Live* and played Len Tukwilla, Driftwood Sculptor? Interviewed by Nora Dunn and Jan Hooks, who were themselves mocking a Lifetime-network chat show called *Attitudes* (which was hilarious in its own right, though not on purpose), Malkovich, who sported a long, blond wig and perched lotus-style on the cushy set chair, used a pitch-perfect slacker cadence to describe his craft. After finding a piece of driftwood, Tukwilla explained, he prepped it by sanding and oiling it. Then, Tukwilla liked to "glue a small squirrel or bird on it."

Creating jewelry can be similarly effortless if you have the right adhesive on hand. In particular, stock up on jeweler's cement, which creates a strong yet flexible bond, and on cyano-acrylic glue (a.k.a. "Super Glue"), which is quick-drying (though tends to be more brittle). I have a special affinity for E6000 adhesive, and not just because breathing it in makes me just a teeny bit woozy. (*Note:* I am in no way advocating sniffing glue here. Relax.) Craft glue can also come in handy, especially if you're working with wood beads or leather cord.

Survival Tools

The Department of Homeland Security has suggested that Americans arm themselves with a variety of survival tools—flashlight, wind-up radio, and, of course, duct tape. As a beader, I'd like to add a few essentials to this list. In this section, you'll find out what no beader's bomb shelter should be without. By the way, make it a point to buy the best beading tools you can afford. In particular, look for implements that have cushy handles and that don't require the hand strength of the Incredible Hulk to operate.

Cut and Run

At the very least, you'll need to get your hands on a pair of beading scissors, which are characterized by sharp blades and a teeny tiny tip to allow for cutting in tight spaces. In addition, you'll absolutely want to invest in a decent set of wire cutters. Be aware, however, that using wire cutters to cut memory wire generally results in a sharp, jagged end—which probably isn't what you're looking for in a bracelet unless you're into self-mutilation. Even if you *are* into self-mutilation (and again, I am in no way encouraging such behavior), you still shouldn't use traditional wire cutters to cut memory wire because your cutters will get chewed up. Instead, spring for special, sturdy, stainless-steel "memory wire cutters." They look like regular wire cutters, but are designed specifically for cutting memory wire. These cutters, which are precision-manufactured using high-quality steel, feature cushion-gripped handles and a built-in spring for comfort and ease of use, and result in a smooth cut.

Big Fat Pliers

If your jewelry oeuvre will involve wirework—hell, even if it won't—you'll absolutely need the following flavors of pliers:

- **Chain nose pliers.** Chain nose pliers look a lot like plain old needle nose pliers found in every hardware store on the planet; both types have "noses" that are flat on one side. The main difference between the two types is the inside of the schnozz on chain nose pliers is smooth, whereas needle nose pliers are roughed up a bit on the inside for better grip. Because that roughness on the needle nose pliers can scratch, I typically opt for chain nose pliers when I need to bend wire at right angles or open or close a jump ring. By the way, if you plan to do a lot of wire work, I suggest keeping a second pair of chain nose pliers handy—it'll make the process of creating wrapped loops a lot easier.

- **Round nose pliers.** Handy for creating loops and curves, round nose pliers feature smooth, tapered, round, er, jaws (thus begging the question why they aren't named "round jaw pliers"—a discussion for another day, perhaps).

> ### Jig Daddy
>
> A jig can do the work of round nose pliers when it comes to bending wire around. Wire jigs look a bit like cribbage boards—they have a ton of little holes in them, which you plug with bitty pegs. Once the pegs are in place, you then wrap your wire around them to form loops, curves, and other bendy shapes.

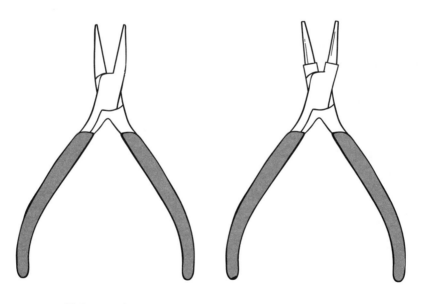

Chain nose pliers   Round nose pliers

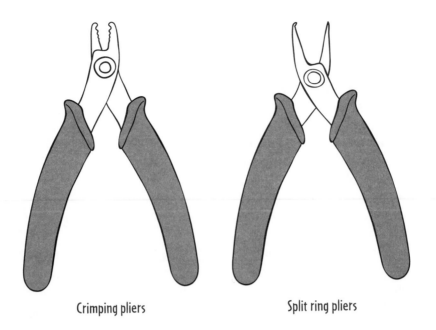

Crimping pliers

Split ring pliers

- **Crimping pliers.** Crimping pliers are used to flatten—can you guess?—crimp beads on your pieces. Although you might be tempted to bypass purchasing crimping pliers and instead use needle nose or chain nose pliers to squish your crimp beads, don't. For one thing, crimping pliers don't damage the thread that's *inside* your crimp bead the way chain nose or needle nose pliers can. Plus, using crimping pliers yields a more professional-looking crimp than needle nose or chain nose pliers do.

- **Split ring pliers.** You know how freaking hard it is to put a key onto a key ring? Actually separating the ends of the ring enough to slide the key on involves the dexterity of an Indian rug weaver, and if you recently had a manicure—well, forget it. Now imagine how much it would suck if that key ring was the size of a ladybug. Hello, exercise in frustration! Here's where split ring pliers come in handy: they enable you to quickly and easily separate the ends of a split ring.

Next!

Now that the important matter of shopping for bead supplies is complete, you're ready to learn what to do with them. The next chapter covers techniques that should be mastered by every beader with a modicum of self respect.

Mandrel in the Wind

One great tool for wirework is a ring mandrel, which enables you to size and form wire into ring shanks. If you intend to make wire-based rings part of your beading repertoire, invest in a ring mandrel; they can be cheaply acquired at most bead stores.

Chapter **Three**

◆■◆

Bead It

Y ou've spent a small fortune on beads and supplies; now it's time to put those goodies to use. In this chapter you'll learn about the basic beading techniques you'll want to master.

The Anal-Retentive Beader: Preparing Your Environment

Remember Phil Hartman (may he rest in peace) as Gene, the Anal-Retentive Chef, on *Saturday Night Live?* He spent the whole sketch *preparing* to cook—cleaning the cook surface, tidying the countertop, ensuring that his peppers were chopped just so—but never actually managed to place a single pot in the oven. Although Gene might have taken things a little far, he may have had a point. At the risk of sounding like an anal-retentive beader, I do suggest you take some time to prepare your work environment for best results. Just don't get so carried away that you never manage to start—let alone finish—your piece.

Destination Organization

As soon as you accumulate even a modest collection of beads, you'll see the need to keep them organized. Failure to implement some type of system results in chaos; unless you're an anarchist—and you know who you are—you'll go mad.

As for me, I'm a capitalist—the nice kind who cares about workers and people in poor countries, not the kind that is intent on destroying the environment and oppressing the masses. This means I understand why our civilization has yielded the sale of specialized bead containers. Although these work great, you can bet that a specialized beading container will put you back more than a comparable item at Lowe's, Home Depot, or Jim's Rod and Reel Deals. (Tackle boxes are especially handy for organizing your materials.) Regardless of where you buy, look for containers with the following specs:

- Ideally, if you buy multiple containers (or plan to add to your single container in the future), look for stackable caddies.

- Make it a point to buy clear containers. That way, you won't have to open each caddy when you're looking for that single gem of a bead you bought 4 years ago but forgot about until just now.

- If you opt for a nonspecialized container for your beads, make sure you don't trip and buy a caddy with removable interior dividers by accident. Granted, some people like them because they enable you to shrink or enlarge the various compartments, but those people are just wrong. Or maybe they're just more capable than I am; I always end up pulling the dividers out by accident and watching in horror as my carefully organized seed beads, categorized by size *and* color, intermingle.

- Never throw away a used Altoid tin, Tic-Tac box, film canister, or prescription bottle. These make great containers for needles and various other beading-related doo-dads.

- You know how cosmetic companies inevitably include a makeup bag whenever they run a "gift with purchase" promotion? Those bags are great for housing your beading tools—wire cutters, pliers, and what have you. If you just can't wait for the next Clinique Bonus Time, hoof it to your local Walgreens to buy an el cheap-o cosmetic bag. If the bag is clear, all the better; you'll be able to see what's inside without having to open it up.

Of course, when it comes to organization, storage isn't your only concern. You'll also want some system of organization when you actually begin working on your pieces. Put another way, a tidy workstation is a happy workstation. To that end, consider the following:

- Pay attention! This is essential! Invest in a bead mat—a small piece of sponge-y fabric—for your work surface. Then, as you work on your project, make it a point to keep your loose beads on it so they don't all wind up on the floor. It will be the best $2.85 you've ever spent in your life.

- When beginning a project, avoid the temptation to dump your entire bead collection onto your work surface. Instead, consider which specific beads you want to use and dump only *those* beads. Otherwise, you'll find yourself overwhelmed—which might be okay since you won't have any room to actually work on a piece anyway. Likewise, limit the tools, thread, and findings on your workspace to the ones you actually plan to use.

- Plastic snack trays—the kind with little dividers so your kid doesn't suffer cardiac arrest when his ketchup fuses with his alphabet chicken nuggets—are great for holding your supplies as you work. Ditto those thick paper plates that segregate your baked beans from your potato salad, recycled frozen dinner trays, ice cube trays, utensil trays, muffin tins (if you use paper muffin cups, you'll be able to easily pour unused beads back into their containers), sushi boxes, or deviled egg trays.

♦ Do not—I repeat, do *not*—let your cat on your work surface. She will not understand the critical difference between "$40 glass bead" and "exciting breakable toy."

Get Comfy

Regardless of what activity I'm about to engage in, I take steps to ensure my own physical comfort. If, for example, I'm jetting to, say, Des Moines, that means carting along an extra bag with a travel pillow, sleeping mask, spritzer with Evian, earplugs for drowning out any chatty types nearby, and a stun gun for use on the offending talker in the event the earplugs are ineffective. (Just kidding about the whole stun gun thing.)

Likewise, you should take steps to ensure your physical comfort when beading. In particular, you'll want to make sure your workstation has adequate lighting; this not only helps you see your piece but also prevents the development of crow's feet around your eyes due to squinting—and we can't have those, CAN WE? (Keeping a magnifying glass handy isn't a bad idea either, for the same reason.) Also, ensure that your seat (your chair, not your derrière) has adequate cushion for your seat (your derrière, not your chair). Finally, good posture is key. That's not to say you should bead with a book on your head, but do make an effort to sit up straight. Your back—and your cotillion instructor—will thank you.

String 'Em Along: Basic Bead Stringing

You probably learned how to string beads around the same time you discovered the wonders of Jell-O, so I'm guessing I don't have to delve into the fundamentals. (Using scissors, cut thread. Using fingers, pick up bead. Feed thread through the hole in the bead. Yaaaay!) That said, stringing actual necklaces or bracelets, as opposed to just disembodied ropes of beads, does require a bit more know-how.

Designing Women

For one, the adult in you is probably a bit more concerned with design than the toddler in you was. That means considering these points before you put bead to string:

♦ Do you want your piece to include beads that appear in a pattern, or beads that are interspersed randomly throughout?

♦ Do you want your piece to be symmetrical or asymmetrical?

♦ Do you want your piece to involve a focus bead—that is, a single bead that draws attention, which may or may not be complemented by additional beads?

- Do you want your piece to be textured or smooth? This may dictate the types of beads you select.
- How many and what colors do you want to use? If you plan to use multiple colors, you might want to research color theory at least a little so you don't wonder why your key-lime green focus bead looks hideous next to your burnt sienna and periwinkle complements.

One way to explore color theory without forking over art-school tuition is to park yourself in front of a display of paint chips at your local hardware store—especially the ones created by interior designers to demonstrate which diverse colors work well together. Next time you hit your local bead shop, go armed with the paint chips that really caught your eye in the hopes of finding beads that match. Beyond that, look to fashion, food, and home magazines for color-combination ideas. A color wheel can also be a good tool for choosing colors.

If you find yourself repeatedly trashing pieces after stringing them because they don't look *just so*, consider investing $6 on a bead board. These nifty plastic trays are texturized to prevent your beads from escaping, and feature channels to house your beads as you plot your piece. Each channel is ticked with measurement markers to help you make sure the bracelet

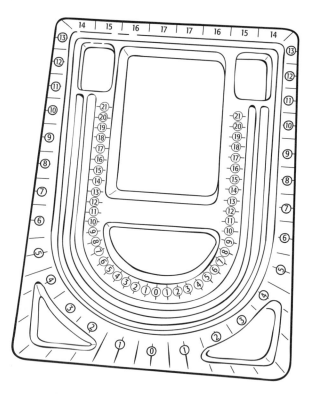

Using a bead board, also called a "design board," makes laying out your design a breeze.

The Long and the Short of It

To help you determine how long your piece should be, here are some standard lengths:

- Choker: 16 inches (women) or 18 inches (men)
- Pendant length: 18 inches (women) or 20 inches (men)
- "Matinee" length (just above your décolletage): 20-24 inches
- "Opera" length (just below your sternum): 28-32 inches
- Rope: 40-45 inches
- Lariat (no clasp): 48+ inches
- Bracelet: 6-8 inches (women) or 9-11 inches (men)
- Anklet: 9-10 inches (women) or 11-14 inches (men)

you're making for your twiglike sister won't fall off her wrist; a center marker makes it easy to pinpoint where your focal bead belongs. But wait, there's more! You can stash the beads, findings, and other necessities for your project in the storage compartments carved out of the middle and sides of the board.

Be Prepared

Once you've figured out your piece's design, you're ready to go to town, assuming you've gathered all your project-related components. Specifically, you'll need the following:

- Beads
- Thread or beading wire
- Sharp scissors or wire cutters
- A single-strand clasp (that is, a clasp designed for one strand rather than for two or more strands)

If you've opted to use beading wire as your thread, you'll want to make sure it's thin enough to fit through your beads twice (you'll see why in a minute). Also, if you're using beading wire, you'll need two crimp beads and crimping pliers in addition to what I've listed above; these aren't necessary if you've chosen to use braided, nylon, silk, or stretchy thread. For those, you'll want to have a needle handy to expedite the stringing process, as well as two bead tips, a bit of glue, and a corsage pin (again, minus the corsage).

High-Clasp Hooker: Attaching Your Clasp

Now that you've gathered your tools and materials, you're ready to hook your clasp to your thread. First, use sharp scissors or wire cutters to cut your thread or beading wire, respectively, such that it's 6 or 8 inches longer than the piece you intend to make. (As you get better at attaching clasps, you'll be able to use less thread; for now, give yourself some extra wiggle room.) Then attach one end of your clasp to the end of your thread. If you've opted to use beading wire, do the following:

1. String a crimp bead onto your beading wire.

2. Draw the thread through the loop on your clasp and then back through the crimp bead. The short end of the wire should be an inch or so long, and aligned as closely as possible with the long end of the wire.

Attach one end of your clasp before stringing the beads.

3. Imagine that the crimp bead is your ex-boyfriend's face. Then, using either chain nose pliers or crimping pliers, squish the bead flat.

Attaching the clasp to thread is a bit different. Here's the drill:

1. Tie one end of the thread in an overhand knot—which, for those of us who were too trashy for the Girl Scouts, is just your run-of-the-mill, don't-know-how-to-tie-my-shoes-yet knot. Then add a second overhand knot, right on top of the first one.

2. Using your scissors, trim off the excess thread so that your knots are at the very end of your strand.

3. Draw the end of the thread that is knot-free through the hole in one of the bead tips and pull until the knot rests inside the tip's cover.

4. Carefully drop a speck of glue on the knots inside the bead tip.

5. Using your chain nose pliers, close the bead tip around your knots.

6. Feed the loop on the clasp onto the open loop on the bead tip, and then use your chain nose pliers to close the bead tip's loop.

3

Knot your thread twice before stringing the bead tip.

6

Add the clasp.

Bring Out the Crimp

Using crimping pliers is a bit different from using regular ones. It's a two-step process. First, place the crimp bead in the crimping pliers' inner jaw—where its molars are, if you'll excuse the anthropomorphism—and squeeze the handles to fold the crimp bead in half. Then place the crimp bead *on its side* in the tool's outer jaw—its incisors, if you will—and squeeze.

Got the World on a String: Stringing Your Beads

Hokay. You're ready to string your beads. If you're using beading wire, start by feeding the first few beads through both wires—the long wire *and* the excess, or tail. (If your wire is too thick to pass both ends through your beads, consider using larger beads on the ends of your pieces.) Once all the excess wire is concealed by the beads, carry on stringing as normal. If thread is your vehicle, do yourself a favor and use a needle, beading or otherwise, to string your piece. Otherwise you'll spend half the time sucking on the thread to keep it from fraying. Yeah, okay, thread *is* calorie-free and high in fiber, but that doesn't mean you want to ingest it.

Once you've added all the beads, you're ready to attach the piece to the other loop on your clasp. First, unfasten the clasp so that you have a bit more freedom of movement. Then, if you're working with beading wire, do the following:

1. After you finish adding your beads, string a crimp bead onto your piece.

2. Draw the thread through the loop on your clasp and then back through the crimp bead.

3. Prod the thread through the last three or four beads on your piece to help anchor it, and then tug the excess with your chain nose pliers to tighten the loop attaching the clasp to your piece. The goal here is to have as little space as possible between the last bead of your piece and the crimp bead, but to leave enough room between the crimp bead and the clasp so that the clasp has room to breathe a bit. This can take some practice, so don't lose your enthusiasm if it doesn't work quite right on your first try.

4. Again, envision your ex's face and use your crimping pliers to squish the crimp bead.

5. Use your wire cutters to trim the excess thread from your piece.

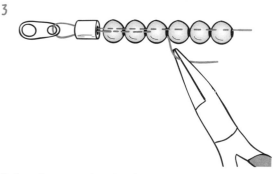

Pull on the excess thread with your chain nose pliers after feeding it through the last few beads of your piece.

When cutting excess wire from your pieces, you can get the closest cut possible by positioning the cutters with the flat part of the cutter toward the work. It works even better when your free hand can pinch the wire and slightly lift the piece up from your work surface, and then cut.

If you used thread rather than beading wire, follow these steps instead:

Add your second bead tip.

1. After you finish adding your beads, string the second bead tip onto your piece. The tip part should face away from the beads you've strung.

2. To ensure that your bead tip doesn't wind up 4 inches from your beads in the final product, tie a loose knot with the remaining thread, and insert the corsage pin or other stabby item through the knot's loop.

3. Grasp the end of the thread with one hand and the corsage pin with the other, and use the corsage pin to prod the knot toward the bead tip. Once the knot is nestled in the tip, pull the thread to tighten it, and then remove the pin.

4. Repeat steps 2 and 3 to add a second knot right on top of the first one, with both knots inside the bead tip.

5. Using your sharp scissors, trim the excess thread from your piece.

6. Squeeze a dot of glue on the new knots.

7. Using your chain nose pliers, close the bead tip around your knots.

8. Feed the loop on the clasp onto the open loop on the bead tip, and then use your chain nose pliers to close the bead tip's loop.

There it is, your first strung piece! If you love it, keep it for yourself. If it didn't turn out quite right, give it to someone you resent.

The Stitchuation Room: Basic Beading Stitches

Don't get me wrong, stringing beads is great. For one thing, it's as easy as persuading a co-ed to show her jugglies on a *Girls Gone Wild* video. Plus, it requires only a minimal attention span. But if you're looking to get into some hard-core beading, the kind that will allow you to win a crafting face-off against Martha Stewart herself, you'll want to learn the basic beading stitches.

Knots Landing

If you're working with particularly pricey beads—think pearls or gems—you might want to make it a point to add a knot between each bead as you work. That way, the next time your paramour rips your necklace from your neck in a fit of passion, your beads won't scatter all over the back seat of your car. Here's how it's done:

1. After you start your strung piece as outlined above—knotting the end, adding a bead tip, and prodding your first bead along to abut it—tie a loose overhand knot.

2. Poke the corsage pin through the loop of the knot.

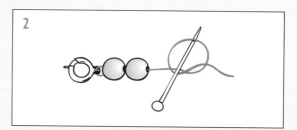

3. Holding the long end of the thread with one hand, use your other hand to draw the pin and knot flush with the bead.

Poke the corsage pin through the loop.

4. With the knot against the bead, extract the corsage pin. Then use your fingers to push the knot against the bead as you pull on the thread to tighten the knot.

5. Repeat for each bead in your piece.

Stitching, or *weaving*, beads involves some degree of skill—not to mention patience—but the results can be stunning.

Before I get into the specifics of how it's done, indulge me as I offer a piece of advice: When learning how to do these various stitches, just make a little scrap rather than shooting for a bracelet or a 2 × 3–foot wall hanging that depicts the Rose Window at Notre Dame. Then, when you've mastered the stitch, you can apply what you've learned to an actual finished piece.

Among the most basic bead stitches are the peyote stitch, the brick stitch, the square stitch, the daisy chain, the ladder stitch, and the right-angle weave, each of which yields a different texture and effect. Regardless of what type of stitch you plan to use, you'll need the following items on hand:

♦ **Beads.** Not to be all Ms. Obvious about it, but you'll need beads—usually seed beads, and typically a specific size and type (i.e., delica or what have you) as dictated by the pattern for your piece. On occasion, you might instead use bugle beads (teeny tiny cylinders), Swarovski crystals, or some other type of uniformly sized bead, depending on the effect you want to achieve.

- **Thread.** As I mentioned in chapter 2, "The Good Buy Girl," thread comes in myriad types, widths, and colors. As with beads, the width you need will depend on what type of piece you are planning to stitch up. Popular types of thread for stitching beads include nylon thread, such as Nymo, C-Lon, and Silamide, or beading wire — specifically FireLine, which acts just like nylon thread but is way stronger. When choosing the thread for your project, make sure you opt for a color that won't clash with your beads.
- **Beeswax (or similar conditioner).** To prevent nylon thread from breaking, fraying, or knotting, keep a bar of beeswax or other thread conditioner handy.
- **Beading needles.** As noted in chapter 2, beading needles differ from plain-old sewing needles in that their eye is the same width as the rest of the needle. This is a particularly helpful feature when working with super-wee seed beads.
- **Band-Aids.** Beading needles can be pretty sharp. Trust me.

Rather than using smaller sizes of seed beads when practicing these stitches, start with larger seed beads — that is, sizes 4, 5, or 6 seed beads, sometimes referred to as "pony beads." That way you don't need to concern yourself with needle size, thread size, and so on. As you begin working on projects that involve stitches, you'll want to refer to the project's instructions to find out what size beads, thread, and needles to use. If no such instructions are given, or if you're winging it, just make sure that the beads you use have big enough holes to allow you to pass the needle and thread through each one a few times.

Look, I'm gonna be straight with you: My coverage of bead stitches barely scratches the surface. There are scores more types of stitches, not to mention variations on variations. Plus, you can really go crazy and learn how to increase and decrease the stitches, much like knitters do, to affect the width of your piece. If you find yourself tapping a vein for more, you'll want to check out any of a number of books devoted solely to beading stitching.

Tension Beadache

Many stitches require the use of a tension bead, a.k.a. *stopper bead*, to ensure that the beads you string on one end of your thread don't slip right off the other end. To make your own tension bead, simply string a bead — any bead — that is larger than the ones in your piece on a length of thread. Then, loop the thread around and pass it through the bead, in the same direction as before, a few more times. Leave yourself a bit of a tail on the short end — 6 inches should do the trick.

Stringing a tension bead.

Smoke It If You Got It: The Flat Peyote Stitch

As a kid, I was profoundly attached to this Navajo-ish belt—you know, the kind with beads strung together in a pattern. Mine had blocky letters spelling "Gatlinburg"—as in Gatlinburg, Tennessee—spanning the back, bound by square-ish girl-type figures on the sides, all stitched onto a leatherette belt tipped with a faux-gold buckle. Admit it—you strapped a similar fashion gem around your 5-year-old tummy. I always wondered how those beads were strung together; turns out, the *flat peyote stitch* was used.

The flat peyote stitch is among the most common stitches used in beading, but it doesn't always involve creating a pattern with the beads—i.e., spelling out "Gatlinburg" or creating a square-ish girl-type figure. If you like, you can just use one color or even various colors in a random pattern. Note, too, that the flat peyote stitch comes in two flavors, even count and odd count, with even count being the easier of the two.

Too Loose? Too Tight? Just Right!

Once upon a time, Goldilocks eschewed breaking and entering the homes of innocent ursidae in favor of beading. She quickly discovered, however, that her thread tension—that is, how tightly her piece was woven—was either too tight or too loose. Turned out she was pulling her thread too hard—or not hard enough—after drawing her needle through beads already attached to her piece. With practice, however, Goldilocks developed a knack for establishing the correct thread tension, and lived happily ever after.

The Even-Count Flat Peyote Stitch

Here's how the even-count flat peyote stitch is done:

1. Since this is just for practice, thread a beading needle with a long strand of waxed nylon thread—a yard should do. After adding a tension bead, string an even number of beads on the thread. In this case, I've strung six seed beads; to make things easy on yourself, I suggest you do the same.

2. Add a seventh bead, and then pull your needle through bead 5. Then add an eighth bead, and pull your needle through bead 3. Finally, add a ninth bead and then pull your needle through bead 1.

1

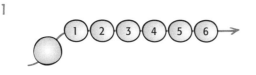

Beginning the even-count flat peyote stitch.

2

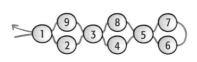

As you add beads 7–9, pull your needle through beads 5, 3, and 1.

3. Add a 10th bead to your piece, and then pull your needle back through bead 9. Add an 11th bead, and pull your needle through bead 8. Finally, add a 12th bead, and then pull your needle through bead 7.

4. Continue in this vein until you've completed several rows.

3

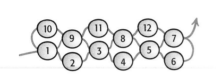

As you add beads 10–12, pull your needle
through beads 9, 8, and 7.

4

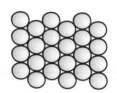

Continue with the stitch until you've completed several rows.

The Odd-Count Flat Peyote Stitch

As I mentioned, the odd-count version of the flat peyote stitch is a bit more treacherous:

1. After threading a beading needle with a long strand of waxed nylon thread — again, a yard should do the trick — add a tension bead and string an odd number of seed beads. In this case, I've strung seven beads; as before, I urge you to do the same during this practice run. So far so good.

1

Beginning the odd-count flat peyote stitch.

2. Add an eighth bead, and then pull your needle through bead 6. Then add a ninth bead, and pull your needle through bead 4. Finally, add a 10th bead and then pull your needle through bead 2. Again, so far so good; except for the addition of the extra bead on each row, this is exactly like the even-count stitch.

2

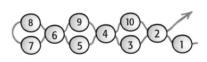

As you add beads 8–10, pull your needle
through beads 6, 4, and 2.

3. Brace yourself! Here's where it gets tricky. Add an 11th bead, and then pull your needle through bead 1 *and bead 2*.

4. After you've pulled your needle through bead 2, loop around the thread between beads 2 and 10, and again pull your needle through beads 2 and 1—but in the opposite direction from before. Then pull the thread back through bead 11. Whew! Glad that's over.

5. Add a 12th bead, and then pull your needle through bead 10. Then add a 13th bead and pull your needle through bead 9. Finally, add a 14th bead and then pull your needle through bead 8.

6. Continue in this vein until you've completed several rows, alternating between the even-count rows and the crazy-ass odd-count rows.

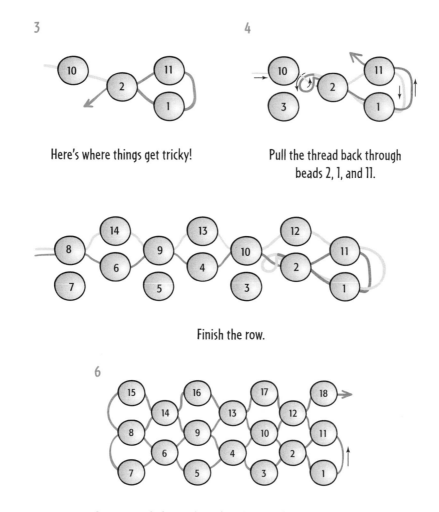

3

Here's where things get tricky!

4

Pull the thread back through beads 2, 1, and 11.

5

Finish the row.

6

Continue with the stitch until you've completed several rows.

Stitch a Brick: The Brick Stitch

The brick stitch differs from the peyote stitch in that the rows are not offset. Instead, the beads line up in the precise horizontal and vertical rows (think the British in 1776). Here are the basics of the brick stitch:

1. After threading a beading needle with a long strand of waxed nylon thread—yet again, a yard should do—and adding a tension bead, use a beading needle to string two seed beads.

2. Using your fingers, situate bead 2 so it is upside-down, side-by-side with bead 1 rather than top-to-bottom.

3. Again pull your needle through beads 1 and 2, in the same direction as before, with the thread exiting from the bottom of bead 2.

4. Add a third bead, pull your needle through bead 2 from bottom to top, and then pull your needle through bead 3 from top to bottom. The thread should exit from the bottom of bead 3.

2

Situate bead 2 so it is upside down,
side by side with bead 1.

3

Loop a second time through
beads 1 and 2.

4

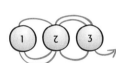

Add a third bead.

5. Add a fourth bead, pull your needle through bead 3 from top to bottom, and then pull your needle through bead 4 from bottom to top.

6. Add a fifth bead, and secure it to the row as with prior beads—pulling your needle back through the previous bead (bead 4) from bottom to top, and then again through the new bead (bead 5) from top to bottom. (Although you can continue in this vein until you simply can't bear it in order to create your first row, I'm calling it quits here.)

5

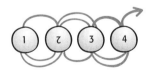

Add a fourth bead.

7. Strengthen and stabilize this first row by pulling your thread back through bead 4 from top to bottom, through bead 3 from bottom to top, through bead 2 from top to bottom, and through bead 1 from bottom to top.

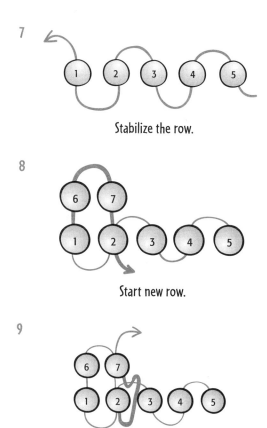

7

Stabilize the row.

8. Begin a new row by stringing a sixth and seventh bead, from bottom to top, situate beads 6 and 7 so they are side-by-side, and pull the needle back down through bead 2 from top to bottom.

8

Start new row.

9. Loop your needle around any of the threads between beads 2 and 3, and come back up through bead 7 from bottom to top.

10. String an eighth bead, situate it so it is side-by-side with bead 7, and pull the needle back down through bead 3 from top to bottom.

9

11. Loop your needle around any of the threads between beads 3 and 4, and come back up through bead 8 from bottom to top.

Loop around the thread between beads 2 and 3.

12. Continue in this vein until you've completed the second row.

13. Continue adding rows, securing each new row to the one that precedes it, until several rows are completed.

It's Hip to Be Square: The Square Stitch

In appearance, the square stitch is quite similar to the brick stitch in that both line up in tidy little rows. But just as twins Elizabeth and Jessica Wakefield of Sweet Valley High fame look exactly alike but have vastly different inner workings, so, too, do the brick and square stitches. Here's how the square stitch is done:

1. After threading a beading needle with a yard-ish of waxed nylon thread and adding a tension bead, string one seed bead.

2. Loop your thread around and pull your needle through the bead a second time, in the same direction.

2

Start your square stitch.

3. String five more beads onto the thread, for a total of six beads.

4. Add a seventh bead, but line it up such that it is below, rather than next to, bead 6.

5. Pull your needle back through bead 6, going in the same direction as before, and continuing on through bead 7 a second time.

6. Add an eighth bead, pull your needle through bead 5 (again, going in the same direction as before), and continue on through bead 8 a second time.

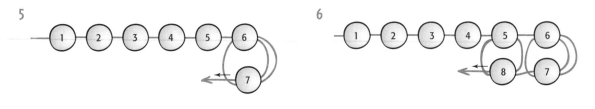

5

Start a new row.

6

Add a second bead to the second row.

7. Add beads 9–12 in the same manner as beads 7 and 8, looping back through the bead above each new bead.

8. After you add bead 12, pull the needle directly through beads 1–6. Do not loop around any beads. Then draw the thread through beads 7–12.

9. Continue in this vein until you have completed several rows. Each time you finish a row, pull your thread through the row above the newly completed row, and then through the new row itself.

8

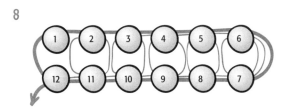

Finish the row.

9

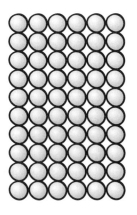

Continue with the stitch until you've finished several rows.

Chain Gang: The Daisy Chain Stitch

The daisy chain stitch represents a shift in that it does not yield a long, hat-bandish strand of woven beads. Rather, the daisy chain resembles, er, a chain of daisies.

1. After threading a beading needle with waxed nylon thread—still using a yard or so, since we're just practicing—and adding a tension bead, string five seed beads of a single color. (I used yellow.) Then add a sixth bead in a contrasting color; I chose pink. The sixth bead will be the center of your first "daisy."

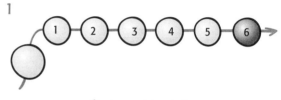

Start your daisy chain.

2. Loop around and pass the needle back through bead 1, in the opposite direction (toward the tension bead).

3. Add three more yellow beads—beads 7–9—and then draw your needle through bead 5. Pull tight to close the circle.

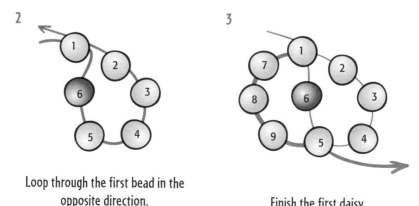

Loop through the first bead in the opposite direction.

Finish the first daisy.

4. String the 10th bead—it should be yellow—and then draw your needle back through bead 9.

5. Add another bead, yellow again, and then draw your needle back through bead 10.

6. String three more yellow beads and one pink bead (beads 12–15), and then draw your needle back through bead 11.

7. Again, string three more yellow beads (beads 16–18), and then pull your needle back through bead 14.

8. Repeat the actions in steps 4–7 to continue adding daisies to the chain.

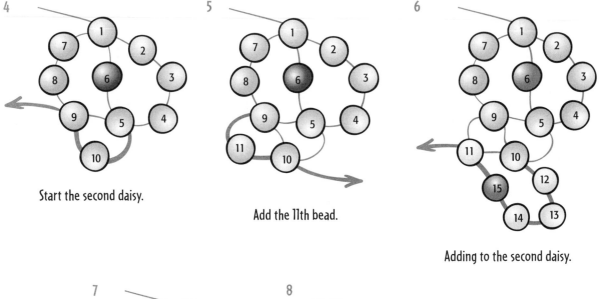

4 Start the second daisy.

5 Add the 11th bead.

6 Adding to the second daisy.

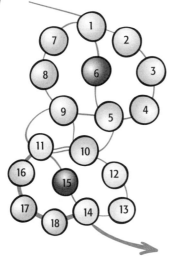

7 Complete the second daisy.

8 Continue adding daisies to the chain.

Ladder Up: The Ladder Stitch

This simple stitch often serves as the foundation for more complicated beading pieces, making it an essential bomb in your beading arsenal. The final product looks a lot like the square stitch and brick stitch, but the process is way less complicated. Here's how it's done:

1. After threading a beading needle with a yard or so of waxed nylon thread and adding a tension bead, string an even number of seed beads (I went with six).
2. For the moment, slide the second half of your strand of beads—in this case, beads 4–6—away from the first half—here, beads 1–3. Then loop your needle around and draw it through beads 1–3 a second time. Pull your thread taut so that beads 4–6 form the second "rung" of your ladder.

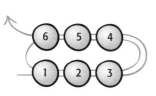

Building the first rungs.

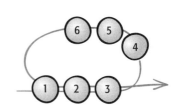

Separate the beads and draw your needle through the first three a second time.

3. Draw your needle through beads 4–6 to anchor the second rung in place.
4. Thread three more beads—beads 7–9—and then loop back around to again draw your needle through beads 4–6.
5. Draw your needle through beads 7–9 to anchor the third rung.

Anchor the second rung.

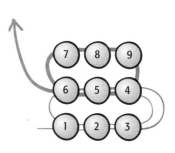

Add the next row.

6. Continue in this vein until you have completed several rows.

7. If after you complete your rows you realize that your piece is as gappy as Elton John's teeth, you can tighten them up by pulling your thread back through each rung, top to bottom—assuming, of course, that the holes in your beads are large enough to accommodate this. If not, better luck next time.

Here's a thought: Try working the ladder stitch with a single bugle bead—they look like itty bitty cylinders—comprising each rung. Be sure to look for bugle beads that are uniform in size. Also, to make sure your thread doesn't get chewed up, look for bugles that aren't all jagged around the edges.

Bead Weaver: The Right Angle Weave

Okay big shot, you've gotten the hang of stitching with a single needle. Now it's time to double up, using two needles *at the same time* for a right-angle weave. Before I start, however, let's lay down some ground rules: When I say "left thread," I'm talking about the thread that is *currently* on the left, not the thread that was *originally* on the left. Ditto right thread, top thread, bottom thread, and so on. Got it? Good. Here's the skinny:

1. Thread one beading needle on each end of a yard or so of waxed nylon thread.

2. Using either needle, string four beads, settling them at the center point of your thread. In this case, I suggest you use the largest seed beads you can get your hands on; they're easier to work with and enable you to see the real effect of the stitch.

3. Cross the left thread through the fourth bead, drawing it through the bead in the opposite direction from the right thread and pulling the string taut (think Brett Favre's buttocks and you'll be on track—if not somewhat distracted). The beads should form a circle-ish, yet cross-ish shape.

4. Add two beads (beads 5 and 6) to the thread on the right.

5. Add one bead (bead 7) to the thread on the left.

6. Cross the left needle through bead 6 and pull the string taut.

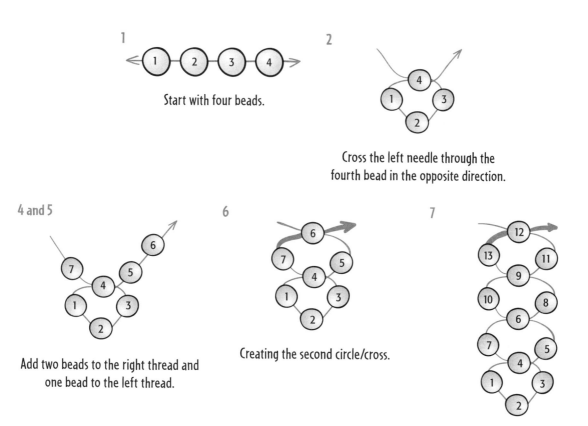

1

Start with four beads.

2

Cross the left needle through the
fourth bead in the opposite direction.

4 and 5

Add two beads to the right thread and
one bead to the left thread.

6

Creating the second circle/cross.

7

Finish the first row.

7. Continue adding circles/crosses in this manner—essentially, weaving figure eights—
   until the row is as wide as you'd like it to be. (I added two more circles/crosses; you
   might want to do the same so you can follow along.)

8. In order to start the second row, you'll need to get your threads in the right place.
   To do so, pull the right thread through bead 11 from top to bottom, and cross the left
   thread through beads 13, 9, and 11 (in the opposite direction of the right thread).

9. To begin the first square of the second row, add two beads (14 and 15) to the top
   thread and one bead (16) to the bottom thread.

10. Cross the top thread through bead 16.

11. Begin adding a second circle/cross to row 2 by stringing two beads (17 and 18) on the
    right thread.

12. Complete the second circle/cross by drawing the left thread down through bead 8 and
    crossing it through bead 18.

13. Continue adding circles/crosses until you have completed the second row, and continue
    adding rows until you've completed several.

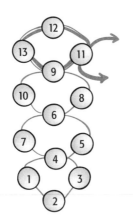
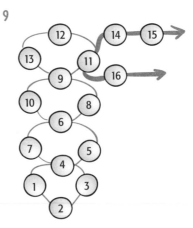

Preparing to start the second row.

Beginning the first circle/cross of the
second row.

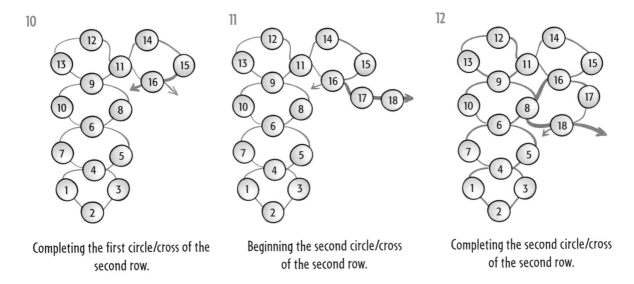

Completing the first circle/cross of the
second row.

Beginning the second circle/cross
of the second row.

Completing the second circle/cross
of the second row.

Feed Your Thread: Adding More Thread to Your Piece

It's inevitable: Someday, somewhere, you'll be three rows away from finishing your piece, only to discover that your thread isn't *quite* long enough. First and foremost, don't get your thong in a knot. You will not be required to start all over with a longer string. Instead, when you have 4–6 inches of thread remaining, tie it off by making a simple knot (not in your thong, but between two beads in your piece). Weave through a few beads already in your piece, pulling

The Pitter Pattern of Little Beads

Once you've mastered your stitches, you might feel up to creating a piece based on a pattern rather than a solid-colored bauble or one that uses a random assortment of beads. Patterns can range from simple—think checkerboard, stripes, or what have you—to incredibly complex—say, a flat peyote stitch bracelet cuff featuring Hieronymus Bosch's *Garden of Earthly Delights*. Beading patterns of all types and stripes can be found online, many free of charge; if you're more reality-based than virtual, peruse the books at your local beading shop.

Of course, you're not *married* to the idea of building your piece based on someone else's pattern. You can always dream up your own patterns either on the fly as you stitch or on paper. You'll find some special pages in appendix B that you can copy to help you plot your designs.

the thread taut to tighten the knot you just made, and then add another knot. After a few knots have been added in this manner, start a new thread by knotting the tail end of it between two *other* beads in your piece and then weave the thread through several beads to return to the point in your piece where you can continue adding beads. Eventually, you'll want to add a bit of Super Glue on these knots; after the glue dries, trim the ends of the threads as short as you can without accidentally cutting your piece, too. (I usually wait until the whole piece is finished to take this step.)

If you run out of thread while working with two needles—say, if you're using a right-

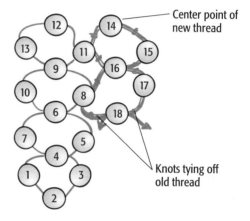

Add more thread to a double-needle stitch.

angle weave—tie off both ends of the existing thread in the manner described in the preceding paragraph. Then, after adding needles to both ends of a new piece of thread, draw the thread through the top bead of one of the circles/crosses you've recently completed, situating the bead at the thread's center point. Weave through the circles/crosses between this bead and the spot where you added the last bead, and pick up from there.

Tie One Off

While I'm on the subject of tying off, I should mention that you'll want to follow the same procedure after you finish stitching a piece so the whole thing doesn't fall apart—a process called "tying off." Just weave back through your piece, making tight little knots as you go. After you've added a few knots, dab a bit of Super Glue on them, wait for it to dry, and then trim the excess thread (again, you don't want to trim so closely that you cut into your piece).

Err Supply: Fixing Your Goofs

While I myself am perfect in every way and never ever make mistakes, I realize that errors of all types are a fact of life for other people, especially my husband. If, as you proceed with a stitched piece, you discover an error in your stitching, you have four choices:

- ◆ Undo all the stitches you've added since the mistake occurred, fix the mistake, and then redo the stitches. If you notice the mistake fairly quickly, this is a reasonable course of action. If you don't notice the mistake you made in the sixth row of your piece until you're on row 31, your attitude about this approach may be somewhat negative.
- ◆ If you simply can't face undoing your stitches, you can use your pliers to crush the problem bead. Then, string your needle with new thread, weave it through several adjoining beads, add a new bead in the empty space you created, and weave through more beads to secure it. Finish by tying off the thread in the usual manner.
- ◆ If you, like me, are a charter member of the Half-Assed Club, you can use a permanent marker to color the offending bead in the correct hue.
- ◆ If no one will notice the problem but you, you can decide to live with it.
- ◆ If the problem is really noticeable but you can't seem to motivate yourself to correct it, you can, as with your sub-par strung pieces, give your second-rate creation to someone you don't like.

Keeping It Together: Attaching a Clasp to a Stitched Piece

Of course, if you actually want to wear a piece you've stitched up, you'll need to add a clasp, be it one you create yourself out of beads and a button, or a sterling silver toggle clasp that you attach. You won't, however, want to wait until you've tightened up the last row of your piece to determine just how to accomplish this. In fact, I suggest you think about how your clasp will be attached *before* you complete your first stitch; that's because some designs call for the clasp to be the very first thing you add to the piece. Alternatively, you may need to build little loops into your beadwork for attaching the clasp after the piece is complete. All this is to say there is no one way to add a clasp to a stitched piece; the method and timing will vary from one design to another. But fear not—you'll learn a few approaches later in this book during Part Two, "Projects."

Wire Wire, Pants on Fire: Beading with Wire

Of course, you're not limited to using thread or beading wire for your projects. As I mentioned in chapter 2, you can also use, er, *wire* wire. In particular, wire can be used as the "thread" for your piece, or it can be used to create your own findings—for example, an eye pin or even a clasp. Chances are, however, that your first brush with wire will be with pre-fab head pins and eye pins when making drop earrings and pendants.

Lieutenant Dangle: Creating Dangles

Now that you've figured out how to string a necklace or bracelet and mastered your stitches, dangles represent the next frontier for the novice beader. Dangles can be attached to ear wires in order to create lovely earrings, to a link of a length of chain in order to create a gorgeous necklace or bracelet (check out the project "Charm School" in chapter 4 to see what I mean), or even to create a ring shank, as in the project "Catch Your Own Bouquet" in chapter 6. Fortunately, making dangles is *way* easy, but does involve some skills I haven't touched on yet—namely, working with wire.

Thanks for the Memories

Perhaps the easiest type of wire to use as "thread" is memory wire because it enables you to string a piece that requires no clasp. Working with memory wire is a breeze—in essence, you just use your memory wire cutters to cut a length (or, more precisely, a circle) of memory wire and slide your beads onto the wire. Of course, you need to create stoppers on each end of the wire to keep your beads from sliding off; to do so, you can glue little memory wire caps onto the ends, or just use your pliers to twist the ends into decorative loops or spirals. (*Be warned:* Memory wire, which is made of steel, can be pretty stiff and is therefore, unlike you, quite resistant to manipulation. Forming it into nifty shapes can require serious strength; unless you're Diamond from *American Gladiators*, expect to suffer a bit.) You'll learn more about how to use memory wire in Part Two, "Projects."

To make a dangle, you'll need the following supplies handy:

- ♦ A head pin
- ♦ A few beads with holes that are large enough to accommodate your head pin
- ♦ Chain nose pliers
- ♦ Round nose pliers
- ♦ Wire cutters

Once you've gathered your supplies, do the following:

1. Prod the head pin through your beads, leaving plenty of room on the top of the head pin free.

2. Holding the chain nose pliers in your dominant hand, grasp the head pin with the tip of the pliers about 1 millimeter above the top bead. Then, use your fingers on your non-dominant hand to bend the wire above the pliers at a 90-degree angle, creating an upside-down L or bent-elbow shape.

3. Position the tip of your round nose pliers in the crook of the "elbow" you created in step 2. (If, every time you loop a head pin, you find yourself dithering over where on the round nose pliers you should wrap the loop, use a permanent marker to indicate on the pliers where the wire should go. That way, you won't end up with dangles that have loops of wildly different sizes.)

4. Using your fingers, curl the wire around the round nose pliers to create a half loop. The wire should be snug around the pliers. To complete the loop, turn the round nose pliers a quarter turn and continue wrapping the wire around them.

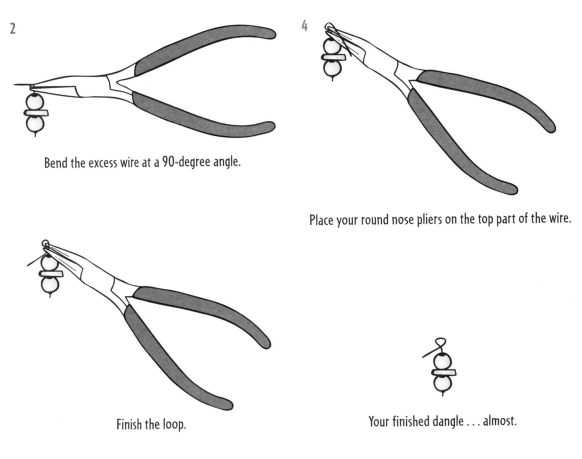

2

Bend the excess wire at a 90-degree angle.

4

Place your round nose pliers on the top part of the wire.

Finish the loop.

Your finished dangle . . . almost.

Loop de Loop: Creating Wrapped Loops

Once you've completed your dangle, you have two options for finishing the loop on top. One is to simply clip the excess wire with your wire cutters, forming an "eye," also called a "simple loop," at the top of the head pin. (This loop acts like a jump ring in that you use your chain nose pliers to open and close it sideways in order to hook the dangle onto, say, an ear wire, a chain, a jump ring, or some other component of your piece.) Simple loops are great in that they don't take much time to create. The other is to wrap the excess wire around the stem of the dangle—that is, the millimeter of wire between the top bead and the loop (hence its name, the "wrapped loop"). While creating wrapped loops is a bit more time consuming, they do allow for a much more secure connection. Here's how it's done:

1. With your chain nose pliers in your non-dominant hand, firmly grip the dangle you just created such that the beads are horizontal and the excess wire crosses behind the stem of the head pin, pointing upward.

2. If you followed my sage advice in chapter 2 and purchased an extra set of chain nose pliers, use that second set of pliers in your dominant hand to grab the end of the excess wire. (If you cheaped out on the second set of pliers, just use your fingers.)

3. Pull the second set of pliers toward you and down, under the stem of the dangle, and back up to their original position to wrap the excess wire around the stem. The wrapped bit should be tight, and as close to the loop as possible.

4. Repeat step 3 as many times as necessary to cover the exposed portion of the stem.

5. Use wire cutters to trim any excess wire. Then, to ensure that the sharp edge of the wire you just cut doesn't pierce the skin of the person wearing your piece, causing her to bleed all over your living room floor and thereby ruin your beautiful antique Persian rug, which your favorite aunt left you when she died, use the chain nose pliers to flatten any protruding wire.

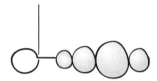

Situate your dangle this way.

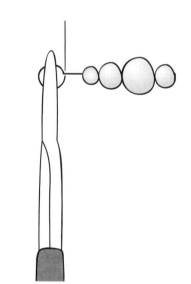

Firmly grasp the dangle with the chain nose pliers.

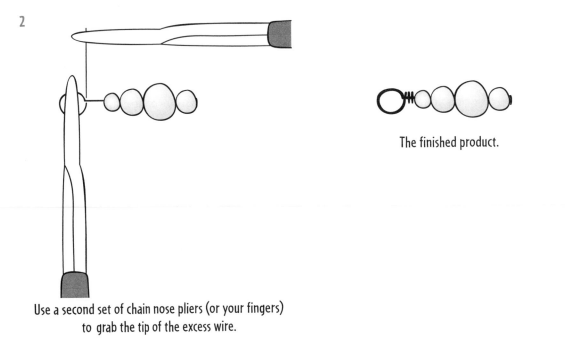

2

The finished product.

Use a second set of chain nose pliers (or your fingers)
to grab the tip of the excess wire.

Of course, you're not limited to creating wrapped loops to make a dangle. You can also create a wrapped loop on one end of a length of wire, add a few beads, and create a second wrapped loop on the *other* end of said length to create a *bead connector* or *link*. You can then connect a series of these links to create a kick-ass necklace.

Hook the second link onto the first one before wrapping
the second loop on the second link.

The trick is to avoid wrapping the second loop on subsequent links until after you've hooked the link onto the one that precedes it. You'll use this technique in the project titled "Financial Freedom" in chapter 4, as well as in "Swinging from the Chandeliers" in chapter 6.

Go Findings Yourself: Creating Your Own Findings

If you're a Bob Vila type, you're probably intrigued by the idea of making your own findings as opposed to going the pre-fab route—especially considering how easy and inexpensive it can be. Take clasps, for example. Clasps, especially if they're purty, can put a dent in the ol' pocketbook. If you're particularly crafty, or just cheap, you might consider making your own. In particular, making toggle clasps is a piece of cake; all you need is a couple bits of 16-gauge (or higher) wire and some round nose pliers.

1. Using the round nose pliers, artfully shape one bit of the wire such that it resembles a lopsided figure eight—that is, with one large loop and one small one. (The key word here is "artfully.")

2. Fashion the other bit of wire into a bar with a small loop in the middle.

3. Trim the bar so that it's at least ¼ inch longer than the opening in the first piece is wide.

4. Use very coarse sandpaper to smooth the edges.

5. If you really want to go crazy, track down a flat-head hammer and an anvil or bench block and pound the bejesus out of both pieces of the clasp until they are flat.

Create a lopsided figure eight.

Fashion a bar with a small loop.

In addition to clasps, you can also fashion your own eye pins, fancy-schmancy head pins, and even your own ear wires. Making eye pins isn't terribly unlike creating a simple loop at the top of a dangle; gussied-up head pins, however, are another matter. For example, to make a spiral-shaped head pin—or, more descriptively, a lollipop head pin—do the following:

1. Use the very tip of round nose pliers to grasp the end of a 6-inch piece of wire; there should be no wire poking out the short side.

2. Using your thumb, press down on the wire as you rotate the pliers a quarter turn. When you can't turn any further, reposition the pliers and continue the rotation to complete a full circle.

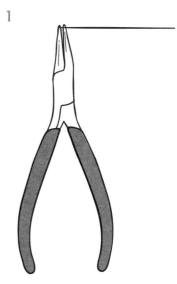

Grasp the end of the wire with the tip of your round nose pliers.

3. Lay the circle flat on the bottom jaw of the chain nose pliers and clamp down. Then, while holding the pliers still, push the tail of the wire against the circle in quarter-turn increments, staying as close to the original curve as possible, to form the "lollipop."

4. After a few complete rotations, position the tip of the chain nose pliers at the point where the lollipop straightens out, and bend the wire at a 90-degree angle.

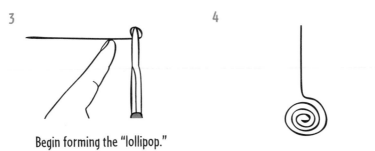

Begin forming the "lollipop."

Finish the lollipop pin.

Another type of handy homemade bead pin is the wrapped-loop pin; simply form a wrapped loop on one end of a length of wire.

Next!

Enough with the boring prelims! You're ready to start making actual, bona-fide pieces. In Part Two, "Projects," you'll learn how to make items ranging from thumbtacks to thumb rings, with necklaces, bracelets, and bobby pins in between.

◆ **Part Two** ◆

Projects

Chapter Four

◆◆◆

Necklace Drivers

Ribbon Campaign

Show your support for style with this fab ribbon necklace.

Financial Freedom

Release yourself from the yoke of debt and instead yoke yourself with this amazing credit-card necklace.

Showcase Showdown

Turn the world on its ear with this upside-down masterpiece.

Charm School

Just because your parents didn't ship you off to finishing school doesn't mean you can't turn on the charm!

Baby You're a Star

You'll look like a star when you wear this gala-worthy beaded piece.

Ribbon Campaign

by Kate Shoup Welsh

You can't hardly fart these days without launching a health-related ribbon campaign. (Puce for Flatulence Awareness!) Although it's enough to tempt a girl to swear off ribbons of all kinds forever, resist! Ribbons are super pretty and can be used to make gorgeous beaded jewelry.

Project Rating: Fling

Cost: $15

Necessary Skills: Bead stringing (page 33)

Materials

- 50 beads (give or take) with large holes (I opted for ones that had a bit of shimmer to them.)
- 4 yd wire-free sheer ribbon, no wider than 7mm
- 1 double-strand clasp (The loops on the clasp should be large enough to allow you to pull the ribbon through twice.)
- Sharp scissors
- Latex gloves
- Super Glue
- Bead mat

1 **Snip** the 4-yd ribbon into two 2-yd parts. (Each segment will be doubled on the necklace, for a total of four strands.)

2 **Apply** Super Glue to one end of one strand of ribbon, and then, while wearing your latex gloves, use your fingers to roll that end of the ribbon to form a point. (Using gloves rather than your bare fingers will go a long way toward ensuring you don't glue your own person to said ribbon.) When the Super Glue hardens,

this end of the ribbon will act like a blunt needle, making it waaaaaay easier to thread the ribbon through the holes on your clasp and in your beads.

3 **Pull** the ribbon, Super Glue end first, through the bottom loop on one end of your clasp, until the tail is about 2 in long.

Pull the ribbon until the tail is about 2 inches long.

4 Using an overhand knot, **attach** the ribbon to the clasp loop. Pull tightly to secure the knot.

5 **String** a dozen or so beads onto the ribbon at random intervals, consuming half the length of the ribbon. (The holes in my beads were small enough that the beads stayed in place; if your beads won't stay put, consider securing them with knots on each side. See the sidebar "Knots Landing" in chapter 3, "Bead It," if you need some guidance.)

6 **Pull** the ribbon through the bottom loop on the other end of the clasp until the beaded portion is long enough to prevent strangulation, but shorter than the remaining ribbon in the strand. Once the length is right, tie an overhand knot to secure the ribbon to the clasp; this will prevent the ribbon from slipping.

8 When you finish stringing beads, **pull** the ribbon through the same loop of the clasp as in step 3. (This might be tight — you've already pulled the ribbon through once. Persevere!)

9 **Tie** an overhand knot to secure this end of the ribbon to the clasp.

6

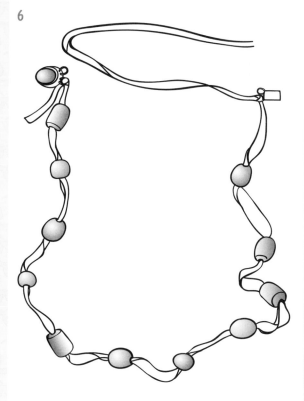

Knot the ribbon onto the clasp to keep it from slipping.

9

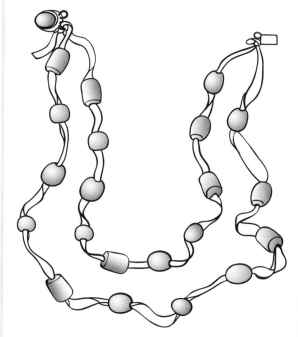

Knot both ends of the ribbon through the same loop.

7 **Repeat** step 5, again stringing the beads at random intervals, but this time use more ribbon to make a slightly longer strand.

10 **Repeat** steps 2–9 with the other 2-yd length of ribbon, attaching it to the top loops of the clasp. You now have a four-strand necklace, with each strand a slightly different length.

11 **Apply** Super Glue to all the knots in the necklace to strengthen the connection.

12 When the Super Glue dries, **snip** the ends of the ribbon as close to the knots as you can get away with.

Variation

Navel Grazing

by Kate Shoup Welsh

A great way to showcase some beautiful ribbon is to wear a particularly long length of it as a navel-grazing necklace, weighted down by some fancy-schmancy charms. To begin, get your hands on an inch-wide key ring (sans keys), and attach several purty dangles to it (I used 11). Then, attach a yard-long length of ribbon (mine was deep red in color and about 8mm wide) to the key ring by folding the ribbon in half to create a loop at the center point. Poke the loop through the key ring, and then poke the ends of the ribbon through the loop and pull tight. Rather than using a clasp to fasten the necklace, just double-knot the ends (make sure the necklace will be long enough to slip on and off over your head). To strengthen the connection, apply a few drops of Super Glue to the knot; after it dries, snip off any excess ribbon.

Financial Freedom

by Laury Henry

When I was 7, my parents took us to Mackinac Island and gave each of us $10 before ditching us for the day. (This was in the 1970s, before the phrase "child neglect" had entered the vernacular.) "Use it wisely," they admonished—the subtext being, "Don't spend it all on fudge." So after careful consideration, I purchased an umbrella hat. Surely they would celebrate my choice; it was useful, after all, able to both shade me from the sun *and* protect me from rain. Sadly, however, they inexplicably viewed it as further proof of my inability to be sensible with money—a view that has been borne out by the fact that I frequently carry more debt than Michael Jackson. Fortunately, this project provides an outlet for all those credit cards I've cut up over the years—and the resulting necklace goes spectacularly with my umbrella hat.

Project Rating: Fling

Cost: $20

Necessary Skills: Wirework (page 55)

Materials

- 36 jump rings or split rings
- 21 glass cane beads in various colors
- 42 crystal bicones, 4mm or 5mm, in various colors
- Toggle clasp
- 6–8 ft of 22-gauge wire (We used half-hard sterling silver.)
- 10 (ish) credit cards, defunct gift cards, or similar items in a variety of colors
- 72 eyelets in various colors (Find these in the scrapbooking section of your local craft store.)
- Leather punch (Find this in the leathercraft area of your local craft store.)
- Round nose pliers
- Chain nose pliers
- Split ring pliers (if you opt for split rings over jump rings)
- Wire cutters
- Sharp scissors
- Hammer
- Emery board
- Bead mat

1 **Cut** a 3½-in length of wire and create a wrapped loop on one end, trimming excess wire from the wrapped loop as needed.

2 **Thread** one crystal bicone bead, one glass cane bead, and a second crystal bicone bead onto the wire.

3 **Create** a wrapped loop on the other end of the wire to secure the beads.

3

This is the first "link" of the necklace's chain.

4 **Repeat** steps 1–2 to create a second link.

5 **Attach** the second link to the first link, wrapping the loop on the second link to secure the connection.

5

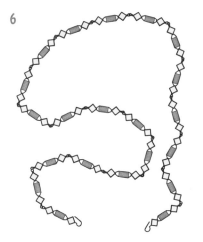

Hook the second link to the first one, and then wrap the excess wire.

6 **Continue** creating additional links and adding them to existing links until you've used all the glass cane beads and crystal bicones, but make sure the last links on both ends of the chain feature hooks rather than wrapped loops so you'll be able to attach the clasp.

6

Make sure you don't wrap the wire at each end of the necklace so you'll be able to attach the clasp.

7 **Attach** the bar portion of the clasp to one end of the necklace and the toggle portion to the other, wrapping the wire loops and snipping off any excess wire.

8 Now for the fun part. Wielding extremely sharp scissors, **slice** and **dice** your credit cards into various shapes and sizes. We opted primarily for rounded rectangles and triangles. You'll need 72 pieces in all.

9 Using the emery board, **file** the sharp points on your credit-card pieces to blunt them. That way, your necklace won't stab you in the jugular. When you're finished, file your fingernails; pretty hands are happy hands!

10 Using the leather punch, **punch** a hole into the top of each credit-card piece.

11 **Hammer** an eyelet into the hole in each credit-card piece.

12 **Attach** two credit-card pieces to each jump ring or split ring; you should wind up with 36 dangles.

13 **Attach** a credit-card dangle to one of the wire loops that connects the second link of the chain to the third one.

13

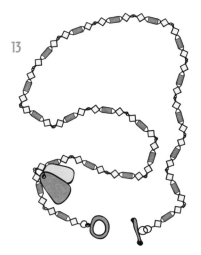

Attach the first credit-card dangle to the chain.

14 **Attach** a credit-card dangle to one of the wire loops that connects the third link of the chain to the fourth one.

15 **Connect** the remaining credit-card dangles to the wire loops that separate the links, working toward the other end of the necklace, until all the dangles have been attached.

Variation

Extra Credit

by Laury Henry

French ear wires: 41¢. Two eyelets: 12¢. Making earrings from your cancelled Visa cards: Priceless. Simply cut out the Visa logos on two of your credit cards, use your leather punch to create the necessary holes, hammer the eyelets in, and attach the plastic pieces to ear wires.

Showcase Showdown

by Charissa Brannen

Traditionalists believe that the clasp goes in the back of your necklace, and the focus, or showcase, bead goes in front—no exceptions. Defying that rule—putting the clasp in front, alongside the focus bead—can be your subtle way of sticking it to the man. Okay, maybe not sticking it to the man, but definitely sticking it to Anna Wintour. Plus, it ensures that the kick-ass clasp that consumed half your beading budget will be noticed by all.

Project Rating: Fling

Cost: $15–$25, depending on your materials

Necessary Skills: Bead stringing (page 33), wire-work (page 55)

Materials

- 1 oval-shaped stone, 20–25mm (We went with turquoise) with a top-to-bottom hole through the center
- 1 faceted stone, 6mm (We chose carnelian.)
- 3 sterling silver flower spacer beads, 5mm
- 1 sterling silver head pin, 3 in
- 1 length of multi-strand beading wire, à la Beadalon, SoftFlex, or what have you, 18in
- 1 small sterling silver toggle
- 2 crimp beads
- 2 sterling silver balls, 4mm
- Approximately 170 sterling silver balls, 3mm (assuming a coverage of 10 balls per in)
- Chain nose pliers
- Round nose pliers
- Crimping pliers
- Wire cutters
- Bead mat

1 **Slip** the 3-in head pin through the hole in the large oval stone.

2 **Add** the spacer beads to the head pin, followed by the 6mm faceted stone.

3 **Begin** forming a wrapped loop with the excess wire at the top of the head pin, but stop at the point that the wire is shaped like a hook.

4 **Slip** the toggle portion of the clasp onto the hook.

4

Attach the dangle to the toggle portion of the clasp.

5 **Complete** the wrapped loop. When you're finished, you should have a pendant hanging from the toggle.

6 Using a crimp bead, **attach** one end of your beading wire to the toggle, and use wire cutters to **trim** the excess tail.

6

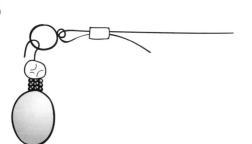

Attach the thread to the clasp.

7 **Begin** the tedious task of beading the remaining 17 in of wire, starting with the 4mm ball bead to hide the exposed end of the cut wire.

8 **String** the 3mm ball beads on the wire until there's about 1 in of wire remaining.

9 **Add** the remaining 4mm bead.

10 Using the remaining crimp bead, **attach** the bar end of the toggle clasp.

Variation

Lariats of Fire

by Charissa Brannen

In the old days, a *lariat* was a rope with a noose, used to lasso up livestock. These days, a lariat is a lovely necklace. Some lariats are simply long ropes of beads whose ends can be loosely knotted or even tossed saucily over one shoulder, as with a scarf. Other lariats, similar to the Showcase Showdown piece, feature a closure in the front. The difference? Rather than using a clasp, a lariat uses single loop–either the loop of a toggle clasp minus the bar or a loop built into the necklace with beads and thread. The other end of the lariat can then be pulled through this loop and left to dangle, like a flashing neon arrow down your décolletage.

Making a looped lariat is simple enough. We used two 6mm faceted pyrite beads, one 3mm faceted sterling silver bead, three 8mm faceted beads, seven sterling silver spacer beads, three 8mm bead caps, one 3 in head pin, one 12mm faceted crystal bead, and approximately 170 2.5mm sterling silver faceted round beads. We strung these goodies on 18½ in of SoftFlex multi-strand beading wire (Beadalon would be fine too), and used two 2mm crimp beads to hold everything together. (Although a lariat is technically supposed to be long–some say if it ain't 48 in, it ain't a lariat–we think rules are for suckers. If you want your rope to be shorter, we won't hold it against you. The one we made is closer in length to a choker, and so far we have eluded the jewelry police.)

continued

continued

We created the dangle first, slipping a bead cap onto the head pin followed by the 12mm crystal bead and one more bead cap, and finishing with a wrapped loop, nipping the excess wire as close as possible.

After setting the dangle aside, we began the "rope" portion of the lariat, forming a loop on one end of the beading wire by stringing one crimp bead followed by 18 2.5mm sterling silver faceted beads. After stringing the last faceted bead, we pulled the beading wire back through the crimp bead to form a $\frac{3}{4}$-in loop with a $\frac{1}{2}$-in tail, give or take a tick. (If the bead on your dangle is larger or smaller than 12mm, you'll need to adjust the size of this loop accordingly.) We used crimping pliers to squish the crimp bead, and used our wire cutters to snip the tail.

Form a loop on one end of the lariat.

Next, we strung the 3mm sterling silver bead onto the beading wire; this hid the crimp bead securing the lariat loop, creating a more finished appearance. Then we strung the remaining 2.5mm sterling silver beads until we had created a strand roughly $13\frac{1}{2}$ in long, with 4 in of wire remaining. We added the remaining beads: one 6mm faceted crystal, one sterling silver spacer bead, one 6mm faceted crystal, three sterling silver spacer beads, one 8mm faceted crystal, three sterling silver spacer beads, one 8mm faceted crystal, three sterling silver spacer beads, one 8mm faceted crystal, and the remaining bead cap. We pulled the end of the strand through the loop on the other end, added a crimp bead, and then attached the dangle. After squishing the crimp bead and snipping the excess beading wire, we were ready to ride.

Charm School

by Terri Hanson

You wouldn't guess it from his flagrant public burps, but my husband actually attended charm school during junior high. He learned which fork is which (not so handy these days, considering that Taco Bell seems to be our date-night destination of choice), a simple box step, and how to properly address his elders. Fortunately, this charm school isn't like *that* one; although you might not be prepared to dine with the queen when you graduate from *our* cotillion, you will have a lovely necklace to show for your efforts.

Project Rating: Fling

Cost: Expect to spend a ballpark figure of $25, depending on what materials you choose

Necessary Skills: Wirework (page 55)

Materials

- 15¼ in of 4.9mm oxidized, textured, patterned chain (We used Rio Grande product number 695-644/B.)
- 1 lobster clasp, 13.5mm
- 49 sterling silver head pins, 2 in
- 49 assorted pearls, semi-precious stones, and Swarovski crystals of varying shapes, sizes, and colors (The mixture shown here includes rhodonite, smoky quartz, fiber optics, coin pearls, freshwater pearls, Swarovski glass pearls, and Swarovski crystals, but feel free to be creative with your own mixture, blending different shapes, sizes, and textures.)
- 2 sterling silver seamless balls for each of the larger beads you select, 2mm
- 1 small sterling silver bead
- Wire cutters
- Chain nose pliers
- Round nose pliers
- Bead mat

1 **Create** your anchor—that is, the dangle that will be affixed to the end of the chain as an accent. To do so, thread one crystal bead followed by one small sterling silver bead on a head pin, and then use a wrapped loop to affix the dangle to the last link on one end of the chain.

2 **Lay out** your beads in the order they will be attached to the chain. We put the larger, more impressive beads toward the center, accompanied by 2mm sterling silver balls, and tapered in at the ends with the smaller beads.

3 Going from left to right, **slide** the first bead onto a head pin, but do not wrap the excess wire (that way, you'll be able to attach the head pin to the chain later). Repeat until all the beads for your necklace are on head pins, making sure to keep the dangles in the proper order as you work. The dangles that house your more impressive stones will also feature two 2mm sterling silver balls—one below the larger bead, and one above it.

3

Create the dangles for the necklace,
but do not wrap the loops.

4 It's easiest to start at the center and work your way outward; to begin, **locate** the center of your chain, and use a wrapped loop to **attach** the center bead.

5 **Continue** attaching the dangles to the chain, working from the center outward, until all are affixed.

6 **Open** the jump ring attached to the lobster clasp sideways, **slip** the clasp onto the end of the chain (not the end with the anchor), and **close** the ring.

Variation

Charm's Cool

by Terri Hanson

If just *thinking* about making all those dangles gives you a hand cramp, consider making a bracelet instead of a necklace. That way, you'll only need 39 dangles instead of 49. (Don't forget to shorten the chain accordingly–7½ in should do the trick. Also, to accommodate the fact that this bracelet will likely have a "tail" when worn–that is, some extra chain hanging off the end after the clasp is engaged–you might want to offset the center bead by 1¼ in or so.) Even better, make earrings. They require only 10 dangles. Here's how:

1. **Collect** two focal beads, ten 2-in sterling silver head pins; four 2mm sterling silver balls; eight 4mm Swarovski Austrian crystals; and two sterling silver French wires.

2. **Thread** a sterling silver ball, a focal bead, and a second sterling silver ball on one head pin, and **repeat** with a second head pin.

3. **Attach** each head pin to a French ear wire and **wrap** the excess wire around the top of the pin.

4. **Slide** one 4mm crystal on one of the remaining head pins.

5. **Create** a simple loop at the top of the head pin, snipping any excess wire.

6. **Repeat** steps 4-5 for the remaining seven head pins and crystals.

7. **Open** the loop at the top of each head pin partway.

8. **Slip** two head pins on the mapped loop on one of the head pins attached to the French ear wire, and two head pins on the French wire's loop.

9. **Close** the loops to secure the dangles onto the earring.

10. **Repeat** steps 8 and 9 to complete the second earring.

Baby You're a Star

by Connie Weber

I'll be honest—this necklace involves a bit of sweat investment. But I swear, it's worth it, if for no other reason than it will make for a spectacular complement to your gown the next time you're invited to a state dinner. By the way, don't feel married to the colors used here; if you read *Color Me Beautiful* in the fourth grade, like I did, and after careful consideration of the cut-out swatches determined that you, too, are a Summer, feel free to select some colors that better suit your palette.

Project Rating: Love o' Your Life

Cost: $40

Necessary Skills: Bead stringing (page 33) and bead stitching (page 38)

Materials

- 6 Swarovski crystal bicones, 8mm (Ours were indicolite, which is sort of teal-y, but we'll call it "color 1" in case you opt for a different set of colors.)
- 10 color 1 Swarovski crystal bicones, 6mm
- 1 Swarovski crystal bicone, 6mm (Ours was Siam double AB, which is purple-ish, but we'll call it "color 2" from here on out.)
- 5 color 1 Swarovski crystal bicones, 4mm
- 12 color 2 Swarovski crystal bicones, 4mm
- 124 color 2 Swarovski crystal bicones, 3mm
- 4 rose montées, 3mm (Ours were bermuda blue. *Be warned:* These can be tricky to find. If you have trouble locating some, you can opt for a regular 3mm bead instead.)
- 2-3 grams size 12 color 1 AB Japanese 3-cuts
- 1-2 grams silver charlottes
- 2 sterling silver clamshell bead tips
- 1 sterling silver jump ring
- 2-3 in sterling link chain
- 1 sterling silver lobster claw clasp
- FireLine thread (6 lb., fine)
- 2 size 12 tapestry needles
- Beeswax or thread conditioner
- Sharp scissors
- Chain nose pliers
- Round nose pliers
- Wire cutters
- Bead mat

Construct the Small Star

The first piece of the necklace you'll build is the five-pointed star that acts as a pendant.

1 **Cut** a 4-yd length of FireLine.

2 **Draw** the length of the thread across the beeswax several times to condition it.

3 **Thread** two size 12 tapestry needles on the FireLine, one on each end.

4 Using one needle, **pick up** one 3-cut Japanese seed bead and **pull** it down to the mid-point of the thread.

5 With both needles, **pick up** the color 2 (in our case, purple) 6mm crystal bicone and another 3-cut Japanese seed bead. **Pull** both down to sit on top of the first seed bead. This constitutes the bottom of the necklace.

6 Put the left needle in the left side and the right needle in the right side of a 4mm color 1 (here, teal) crystal bicone and **cross through** the bead. Pull evenly until the crystal sits with its bicone ridge centered on the seed bead below.

7 With the right needle, **pick up** a seed bead, followed by two 3mm crystal bicones in color 2.

8 With the left needle, **pick up** a seed bead, two 3mm crystals in color 2, and a second seed bead.

9 Using the left needle, **cross through** both 3mm crystals on the right needle (you'll be going through the beads in the opposite direction from the right needle) and **pull tight**.

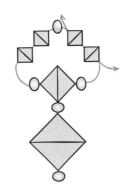

Cross through the 3mm crystals on the right needle.

10 **Point** the bottom of the necklace to the right, at 3 o'clock. Then, with the right needle, **pick up** a seed bead, a 4mm crystal bicone in color 1, and another seed bead.

11 With the left needle, **pick up** a seed bead, followed by two 3mm crystals in color 2.

12 Using the right needle, **cross through** both 3mm crystals on the left needle and **pull tight**.

13 **Point** the bottom of the necklace toward you, at 6 o'clock. Then **repeat** steps 10–12.

14 **Point** the 6mm bicone slightly to the left, at 8 o'clock. Then **repeat** steps 10–12 a second time.

15 Point the 6mm bicone toward you. With the needle currently at the center of the star, **pick up** a single seed bead, and then **draw** the needle through the row of 3mm crystals you added in step 8, starting in the middle of the star and pulling outward.

16 With the other needle, **pick up** a seed bead, a 4mm bicone in color 1, and another seed bead.

17 **Cross** the needle used in step 16 through the two 3mm crystals through which you passed the left needle in step 15, but from the outside of the star inward. Your needle will emerge at the center of the star.

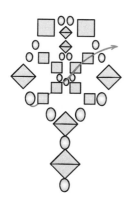

Cross through the adjoining 3mm crystals.

18 With the right needle, **pick up** a rose montée, and then **draw** the needle through the set of 3mm crystals opposite the 6mm crystal at the bottom of the necklace.

19 **Pull** the left needle clockwise through the next seed bead, 4mm bicone, and seed bead, and then through the next set of 3mm crystals toward the center of the star.

20 Still using the same needle, **pass** through the set of 3mm crystal bicones opposite the 6mm bead comprising the bottom of the necklace.

Follow the thread path of the star—through the spokes and the beads on the perimeter that link them—with the left needle.

21 **Pull** the right needle clockwise through the next seed bead, 4mm bicone, and seed bead, and then through the next set of 3mm crystals toward the center of the star. Then **continue** working the same needle in a clockwise fashion, pulling it through the next seed bead and the next set of 3mm crystals, toward the outer portion of the star. Carry on in this manner, working the needle through the seed beads and 4mm bicones on the star's outer ring, through the 2mm bicones toward the center of the star, through the next seed bead, and through the next set of 2mm bicones toward the outer ring. Stop when you pass through the seed bead, 4mm bicone, and seed bead above the 6mm bead at the bottom of the necklace. (Note that the actions you've just taken in this step will turn up like a bad penny in this project; I call it "following the thread path." It's just a way to both strengthen the star you're working on and position your needles for the next step.)

22 **Pull** the right needle through the first set of 3mm crystals from the outside of the star inward. (This is the row of 3mm crystals you added in step 8.)

23 Still using the right needle, **pass** through the set of 3mm crystal bicones opposite the 6mm bead at the bottom of the necklace.

23

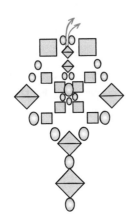

Both needles should emerge at the top of the star from the two 3mm bicones opposite the 6mm crystal.

24 **Pull** both needles through one seed bead, one 3mm bicone in color 2, and another seed bead.

Construct the Large Central Star

The next portion of the necklace you'll construct is a six-pointed star, from which the pendant will dangle.

25 With the right needle, **pick up** a seed bead, an 8mm crystal bicone in color 1 (let's call this the first 8mm crystal), a second seed bead, two 4mm crystal bicones (notice we said 4mm, not 3mm) in color 2, and—wait for it—a third seed bead.

26 With the left needle, **pick up** two 4mm crystal bicones in color 2 and one seed bead.

27 Using the left needle, **cross through** the two 4mm crystals on the right needle and **pull tight**.

28 **Point** the bottom of the necklace toward you and slightly to the left, at 8 o'clock. Then, with the right needle, pick up a seed bead, a second 8mm crystal bicone in color 1, and another seed bead.

29 With the left needle, **pick up** two 4mm crystals in color 2.

30 Using the right needle, **cross through** both 4mm crystals on the left needle and **pull tight**.

31 **Point** the bottom of the necklace to the left, at 9 o'clock. Then, with the right needle, pick up a seed bead, a third 8mm crystal bicone in color 1, and another seed bead.

32 With the left needle, **pick up** a seed bead followed by two 4mm crystals in color 2.

33 Using the right needle, **cross through** both 4mm crystals on the left needle and **pull tight**.

34 **Point** the bottom of the necklace up and to the left, at 11 o'clock, and **repeat** steps 31–33 to add the fourth 8mm crystal to the star.

35 **Repeat** steps 31–33 to add the fifth 8mm crystal to the star.

36 With the left needle, **pick up** a single seed bead, and then **draw** the needle through the first existing row of 4mm crystals (this is the row of 4mm crystals you added in step 26), starting in the middle of the star and pulling outward.

37 **Point** the bottom of the necklace up and to the right, at 1 o'clock, and, with your right needle, **pick up** a seed bead, the sixth 8mm crystal bicone, and another seed bead.

38 **Cross** the right needle through the two 4mm crystals through which you passed the left needle in step 36, but from the outside of the star inward. Your needle will emerge at the center of the star.

39 With the needle currently at the center of the piece, **pick up** a rose montée, and then **draw** the needle through the set of 4mm crystals across from the set you passed through in steps 36 and 38.

40 **Point** the bottom of the necklace to the right, at 3 o'clock, and then **pull** the right needle clockwise through the thread path until the needle emerges from the 4mm bicones between the third and second 8mm crystals, pointing outward, away from the center of the star.

40

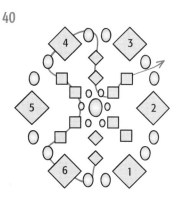

Pull the right needle clockwise around the thread path.

41 With the bottom of the necklace pointing toward you, at 6 o'clock, **pull** the left needle counter-clockwise along the thread path until you've gone all the way around. When you finish, the needle should emerge from the set of 4mm crystal bicones between the third and fourth 8mm crystals.

41

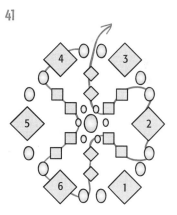

Pull the left needle counter-clockwise around the thread path.

42 **Pull** the left needle through the seed bead on the left side of the third 8mm bead and then through bead 3 itself.

43 **Pull** the right needle through the seed bead on the right side of the third 8mm bead and then through the 8mm bead itself. Both threads should now emerge from the third 8mm bead, but from opposite sides.

String to the Next Star

44 With the left needle, **pick up** three seed beads.

45 With the right needle, **pick up** three seed beads.

46 **Feed** both of your needles through a single charlotte and **pull tight**. **Center** the charlotte over the ridge of the crystal.

47 Using both needles, **pick up** two seed beads, followed by one 3mm crystal in color 2.

48 Using both needles, **pick up** five seed beads or charlottes in any order, followed by one 3mm crystal in color 2. **Continue** adding seed beads, charlottes, and 3mm crystals in this manner until you have six crystals in the sequence (counting the crystal you added in step 47). End with a charlotte.

49 Using the left needle, **pick up** two seed beads.

50 Using the right needle, **pick up** two seed beads.

51 **Add** a color 1 6mm crystal to your right needle, and then **cross through** it with the left needle. **Pull tight** and **center**.

Construct a Medium-Sized Star

Next, build one of the medium-sized five-point stars. This will involve the same basic steps as building the small star that acts as a pendant.

52 **Point** the bottom of the necklace down and to the right, at 4 o'clock. Then, with the right needle, **pick up** a seed bead, followed by two 3mm crystal bicones in color 2.

53 With the left needle, **pick up** a seed bead, two 3mm crystals in color 2, and a second seed bead.

54 Using the left needle, **cross through** both 3mm crystals on the right needle and **pull tight**.

55 With the right needle, **pick up** a seed bead, a 6mm crystal bicone in color 1, and another seed bead.

56 With the left needle, **pick up** a seed bead, followed by two 3mm crystals in color 2.

57 Using the right needle, **cross through** both 3mm crystals on the left needle and **pull tight**.

58 **Point** the bottom of the necklace toward you, at 6 o'clock. Then **repeat** steps 55–57.

59 **Point** the bottom of the necklace slightly to the left, at 8 o'clock. Then **repeat** steps 55–57 a second time.

60 With the left needle, **pick up** a single seed bead, and then **draw**

the needle through the first existing row of 3mm crystals (the ones between the first and fifth 6mm beads), starting in the middle of the star and pulling outward.

61 With the right needle, **pick up** a seed bead, a 6mm bicone in color 1, and another seed bead.

62 **Cross** the right needle through the two 3mm crystals through which you passed the left needle in step 60, but from the outside of the star inward. Your needle will emerge at the center of the star.

63 With the right needle, which is now at the center of the star, **pick up** a seed bead, rose montée, and another seed bead.

64 **Draw** the right needle through the set of 3mm crystals opposite the crystal that's connected to the string of beads that attaches this star to the large central star.

65 Using the left needle, **follow** the thread path in a clockwise manner all the way around the star.

65

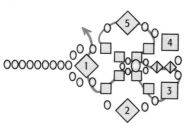

Follow the thread path of the star with the left needle.

66 **Continue** around the thread path with the left needle until it emerges from the row of 3mm crystals separating the fourth 6mm bead from the fifth one. Then, using the right needle, **follow** the thread path in a clockwise manner until the thread emerges from the set of crystals separating the fourth and fifth 6mm crystals.

66

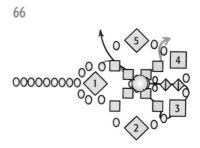

One needle should emerge from the set of crystals separating bead 1 from bead 5, and the other needle should emerge from the set of crystals separating bead 5 from bead 4.

67 **Pull** what is now the left needle through the seed bead on the left side of the fifth 6mm bead and then through the 6mm bead itself.

68 **Pull** what is now the right needle through the seed bead on the right side of the fifth 6mm bead and then through the 6mm bead itself. Both threads should now emerge from the fifth 6mm bead, but from opposite sides.

69 With the left needle, **pick up** two seed beads.

70 With the right needle, **pick up** two seed beads.

71 Feed both of your needles through a single charlotte and **pull tight. Center** the charlotte over the ridge of the crystal.

Continue the String

72 Using both needles, **pick up** one seed bead, followed by one 3mm crystal in color 2.

73 Using both needles, **pick up** five seed beads or charlottes in any order, followed by one color 2 3mm crystal. **Continue** adding seed beads, charlottes, and 3mm crystals in this manner until you have 14 crystals in the sequence (counting the crystal you added in step 72), ending with a series of five seed beads and charlottes.

74 Using both needles, **pick up** a clam shell bead tip, going upward and through the hole at the bottom and through the shell.

75 Using either needle, **pick up** one seed bead.

76 Tie a knot with the threads so that the seed bead is knotted and resting tightly in the clam shell.

77 Draw both needles back down through the hole of the clam shell.

78 Close the clam shell using your chain nose pliers.

79 Draw both needles back down through about 2½ in of beads—7 3mm crystals, and a few additional seed beads or charlottes.

80 Using both needles, **pick up** two seed beads, followed by one 3mm crystal in color 2.

81 Using both needles, **pick up** five seed beads or charlottes in any order, followed by one 3mm crystal in color 2. **Continue** adding seed beads, charlottes, and 3mm crystals in this manner until you have 9 crystals (counting the crystal you added in the previous step)—about 3 in. End with one seed bead and one charlotte.

82 Using the left needle, **pick up** two seed beads.

83 Using the right needle, **pick up** two seed beads.

84 Cross both needles through the fourth 6mm bead in the medium-sized star.

84

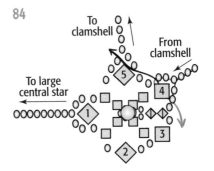

Cross both needles through the fourth 6mm bead.

85 Using your left needle, **follow** the thread path in a clockwise manner, finishing after you pass through the 3mm beads separating bead 1 from bead 2 from the inside of the star outward.

86 **Draw** your right needle through the seed bead to the right of bead 4, through the 3mm beads separating bead 4 from bead 3 from the outside in, and then through the seed beads separating bead 3 from bead 2 from the outside in.

85 and 86

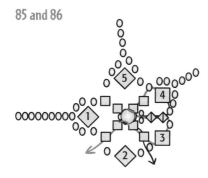

Prepare to string back to the large star.

87 **Pull** the left needle through the seed bead on the left side of the second 6mm bead and then through the 6mm bead itself.

88 **Pull** the right needle through the seed bead on the right side of the second 6mm bead and then through the 6mm bead itself. Both threads should now emerge from the second 6mm bead, but from opposite sides.

89 **Point** the bottom of the necklace away from you and slightly to the left, at 11 o'clock. Then, with the left needle, **pick up** two seed beads.

90 With the right needle, **pick up** two seed beads.

91 **Feed** both of your needles through a single charlotte and **pull tight**.

Center the charlotte over the ridge of the crystal.

92 Using both needles, **pick up** three seed beads, followed by one 3mm crystal in color 2.

93 Using both needles, **pick up** five seed beads or charlottes in any order, followed by one 3mm crystal in color 2. **Continue** adding seed beads, charlottes, and 3mm crystals in this manner until you have 7 crystals (counting the crystal you added in the previous step)—about 2¼ in. end with two seed beads and one charlotte.

94 Using the left needle, **pick up** three seed beads.

95 Using the right needle, **pick up** three seed beads.

96 **Cross** both needles through the second 8mm bead on the central, six-sided star (refer to the figures in the section "Construct the Large Central Star" if you're not sure which bead we mean here).

97 **Point** the bottom of the necklace to the left, at 9 o'clock. Then **draw** your left needle clockwise through the seed bead to the left of bead 2, through the 4mm beads separating bead 2 from bead 1 from the outside of the star inward, and then through the 4mm beads separating bead 1 from bead 6 from the inside of the star outward.

98 **Draw** your right needle through the seed bead to the right of bead 2, through the 4mm beads separating bead 2 from bead 3 from the outside of the star inward, and then through the 4mm beads between beads 2 and 1 from the inside of the star outward.

98

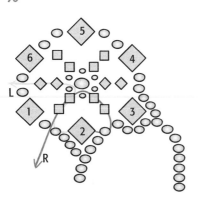

Your threads should emerge on either side of the first 8mm bead.

99 **Pull** the left needle through the seed bead on the left side of the first 8mm bead and then through the 8mm bead itself.

100 **Pull** the right needle through the seed bead on the right side of the first 8mm bead and then through the 8mm bead itself. Both threads should now emerge from the first 6mm bead, but from opposite sides.

101 **Point** the bottom of the necklace toward you and slightly to the left, at 7 o'clock. Then, using the left needle, **pick up** three seed beads.

102 With the right needle, **pick up** three seed beads.

103 **Feed** both of your needles through a single charlotte and

pull tight. **Center** the charlotte over the ridge of the crystal.

104 Using both needles, **pick up** two seed beads, followed by one color 2 3mm crystal.

105 Using both needles, **pick up** five seed beads or charlottes in any order, followed by one color 2 3mm crystal. **Continue** adding seed beads, charlottes, and 3mm crystals in this manner until you have 11 crystals (counting the one you added in the previous step)—about 4 in. End with two seed beads and one charlotte.

106 With the left needle, **pick up** two seed beads.

107 With the right needle, **pick up** two seed beads.

108 **Cross through** the third 6mm bicone in the medium star (this is the only remaining 6mm bicone in the medium star that has not yet been connected to either the central star in the necklace or the clam shell). **Pull tight** and **center**.

109 **Pull** the right needle back through the two seed beads you added in step 106, and then through the string you just created linking the medium star with the main central star, ending by pulling the needle through the three seed beads you added in step 102. The needle should emerge on the left side of the first 8mm bead in the central star.

110 **Pull** the left needle back through the two seed beads you added in step 105, and then through the string you

just created linking the medium star with the main central star, ending by pulling the needle through the three seed beads you added in step 102. The needle should emerge on the right side of the first 8mm bead in the central star.

111 **Cross through** the first 8mm bead in the central star.

112 With the right needle, **follow** the thread path of the star in a counter-clockwise fashion until your needle emerges from the two 4mm crystal bicones between the fourth and fifth 8mm crystal bicones.

113 With the left needle, **follow** the thread path of the star in a clock-wise fashion until your needle emerges from the two 4mm crystal bicones between the third and fourth 8mm crystal bicones.

114

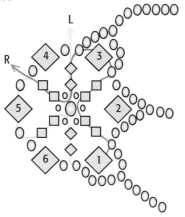

Prepare to begin stringing the other half of the necklace.

114 **Pull** the left needle through the seed bead on the left side of the fourth

8mm bead and then through the 8mm bead itself.

115 **Pull** the right needle through the seed bead on the right side of the fourth 8mm bead and then through the 8mm bead itself. Both threads should now emerge from the fourth 8mm bead, but from opposite sides.

116 That's it—you're finished with the first half of the necklace. Go **down** a few martinis.

Complete the Second Half

117 **Flip** the necklace over so that the back side of the necklace is face up, the bottom of the necklace is pointing toward you, and the clam shell is on your left. That way you can simply mimic the steps you completed to build the first half of the necklace in order to complete the second half.

118 Beginning with the section "String to the Next Star," **repeat** steps 44–64.

119 It's probably occurred to you that the rose montée you just added is on the back side of the necklace. To ensure that it appears on the *front* of the necklace, simply **flip over** the star you've just constructed. (Don't flip the whole necklace; just the star will do.)

120 **Continue** building the second half of the necklace, repeating steps 65–111.

121 Holy mother of God, you're fin-ished stitching. **Tie off** by drawing

both threads back through several stitches, tying several knots along the way to secure the necklace.

122 When you're satisfied that you've secured the necklace, dab some Super Glue on the knots. After the glue dries, carefully **trim** any remaining thread.

Finish the Necklace

123 To one of the clam shell bead tips, **add** 2–3 in of link chain to allow for tightening or loosening of the necklace as needed.

124 To the other clam shell bead tip, **add** a jump ring and a lobster claw clasp.

125 For a finishing touch, **add** a dangle with one or two crystals to the end of the length of chain.

Variation

Special Guest Star Ring

by Kate Shoup Welsh

We liked the large central star in this necklace so much, we decided to showcase it in a ring. To do so, we followed steps 25-39 in the section "Construct the Large Central Star," substituting 8mm Swarovski pearls for the 8mm crystal bicones. When we were finished, we had one thread emerging from the 4mm crystal "spokes" on each side of the star; we then added three 4mm crystals to each thread and enough seed beads to encircle the intended digit. After tying off and snipping the excess thread, we were ready to play Pope.

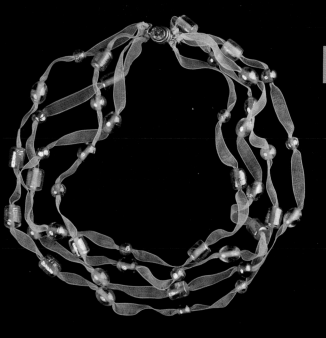

Ribbon Campaign (see page 64)

Showcase Showdown (see page 70)

Financial Freedom (see page 67)

Navel Grazing (variation of
Ribbon Campaign; see page 66)

*Sweater instructions available
in* Not Your Mama's Knitting

Lariats of Fire (variation of
Showcase Showdown; see page 71)

Charm School necklace (see page 73)

Variation: Charm School bracelet and earrings

Special Guest Star (variation of Baby You're a Star; see page 86)

Baby You're a Star
(see page 75)

Doing Time (see page 88)

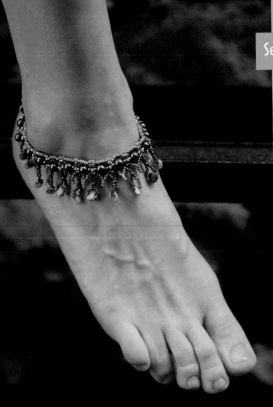

Security Anklet (see page 92)

Choker Face (variation of
Security Anklet; see page 105)

Beadchet Buffet (variation of No Way Crochet; see page 108)

From bottom to top: Doin' the Button (see page 109); No Way Crochet (see page 108); Spiked Punch (see page 119); The Short and Winding Rope (see page 117); Tough Cuff (see page 112)

Billy Idol Called—He Wants His Bracelet Back (variation of Spiked Punch; see page 123)

Far left: Think Small (variation of Doin' the Button; see page 110); Far right: Variation of Spiked Punch (see page 123); Center bracelets: Twisted Sister (variations of The Short and Winding Rope; see page 118)

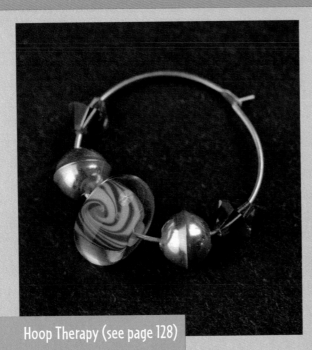

Hoop Therapy (see page 128)

Roll Your Own (variation of Hoop Therapy; see page 128)

Girl with a Curl Earring (see page 129)

Swinging from the Chandeliers (see page 132)

It Curl (variation of Girl with a Curl Earring; see page 131)

Bling a Ding Ring (see page 136)

Play Wristy for Me (variation of
Bling a Ding Ring; see page 137)

Nesting Instinct
(see page 138)
Variation: Nest Obsessed earrings

Toe Rings (variation of
Bling a Ding Ring; see page 136)

Bead the Ball (see page 141)

Nice Stems (variation of Catch Your Own Bouquet; see page 147)

Catch Your Own Bouquet (see page 144)

Hair Tactics (see page 149)

Snobby Pins (variation of
Hair Tactics; see page 150)

Wifebeader (see page 151)

Zip It (see page 154)

Cuff Drops (see page 156)

Handbagger Helper
(see page 158)

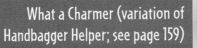
What a Charmer (variation of Handbagger Helper; see page 159)

Call Me! (see page 160)

Girls Gone Bridaled (see page 162)
Variation: Scepter Sold Separately

Know Your Place (see page 169)

Tipple Rings (see page 171)

What's the Stitch? (variation of Tipple Rings; see page 172)

Hit the Bottle (see page 173)
Variation: Pop Your Cork

Serviette Yourself (see page 175)

Tacky Tacky (see page 176)

Original artwork courtesy Troy Cummings

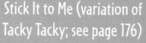

Stick It to Me (variation of
Tacky Tacky; see page 176)

Glass Ceiling Fan Pull
(see page 177)

Kick Ball Chain (variation of
Glass Ceiling Fan Pull; see page 179)

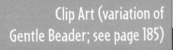
Clip Art (variation of Gentle Beader; see page 185)

The Collar Purple (see page 180)

Gentle Beader (see page 183)

Chapter Five

◆◆◆

Cuff Stuff

Doing Time

The passage of time isn't just about getting wrinkles and crow's feet. It can also be about wearing this gorgeous watch.

Security Anklet

Highlight your dainty ankle with this Turk-inspired anklet!

No Way Crochet

Crochet's not for grannies anymore! Knot up a gorgeous wire bracelet.

Doin' the Button

If your ass is as unsubstantial as mine, "doin' the butt" is out of the question. Not so "Doin' the Button," however!

Tough Cuff

This cuff's as cool as Wonder Woman's—though its bullet-deflecting powers remain untested.

The Short and Winding Rope

Rope yourself into making this sweet leather bracelet. You'll be glad you did!

Spiked Punch

Release your inner punk with this spiked sparkler.

Doing Time

by Rachel Nelson-Smith

I know, I know, wearing a watch means you don't have an excuse to initiate a conversation with that cute guy on the subway by asking him what time it is. But this watch is so flippin' sweet, odds are *he'll* ask *you* where you got it. Think of how impressed he'll be when you tell him you made it with your own two hands.

Project Rating: Flirtation

Cost: $30 (a bit less if you opt for faceted glass beads instead of Swarovski crystals)

Necessary Skills: Bead stringing (page 33)

Materials

- 1 copper watch face with triangular-ish jump rings attached via small loops to the top and bottom (If you rully rully want to use a watch face that doesn't have the jump rings mentioned here, don't freak out—you can make and attach some yourself. We'll show you how. That said, if you know what's good for you, *don't* go for a watch face that has spring-loaded bars.)
- 6 in of 18-gauge copper wire (This is only if you need to make jump rings to attach to the watch face, as mentioned in the preceding bullet.)
- 8 small turquoise-colored beads (You'll string these on copper head pins to create dangles.)
- 8 copper-colored crystal bicones, 4mm (We used Swarovskis. You'll string these on copper head pins to create dangles.)
- 6 copper-colored crystal princess-cut beads, 6mm (We used Swarovskis.)
- 4 copper-colored crystal princess-cut beads, 8mm (We used Swarovskis.)
- Various turquoise glass beads
- Various copper spacer beads and bead caps

- 16 round copper beads, 3mm
- 1 copper 2-strand toggle clasp (If you can't track down a 2-strand clasp, opt for a 1-strand clasp, but make only 3 strands of beads for the watchband rather than 4.)
- 3 ft of flexible beading wire with a diameter of .014 or .015 in
- 16 copper crimp beads
- 16 copper head pins, 20 gauge (If you want to, you can make these yourself using 20-gauge copper wire.)
- 16 copper jump rings, 4mm
- Chain nose pliers
- Round nose pliers
- Crimping pliers
- Wire cutters
- Tape measure or ruler
- Bead mat

Make the Triangular Jump Rings (Optional)

1 If your watch face is *sans* triangular jump rings, you can make your own. To begin, **hold** one end of the 18-gauge copper wire with the middle of your chain nose pliers (as opposed to clamping down with the wire with the pliers' tips or in the deepest part of the pliers' prongs), and **bend** the wire 45 degrees away from you.

2. Use the middle of the chain nose pliers to **grasp** the wire just below the bend you created in step 1, and again **bend** the wire away from you at a 45-degree angle.

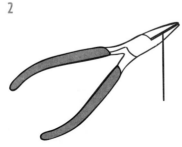

2

Grasp the wire just below the bend.

3. Use the middle of your chain nose pliers to **grasp** the wire just after the bend you created in step 2, and again **bend** the wire away from you at a 45-degree angle.

4. Using wire cutters, **cut** the remaining wire where it overlaps with the first end.

4

You've created the triangular jump ring!

5. Holding one of the ends with the tip of your pliers, **pull** the wire until the ends meet.

6. **Repeat** steps 1–5 to create the second triangular jump ring.

7. **Attach** the triangular jump ring to one of the loops on the watch face such that the opening in the ring is inside the loop.

8. **Repeat** step 7 to attach the other triangular jump ring to the watch face.

Construct the Band

9. Using a crimp bead and your crimping pliers, **attach** one end of the 3-ft length of flexible beading wire to one of the watch face's triangular loops. (Yes, before you bother asking, you should use the whole piece of flexible beading wire to start with.)

10. **Measure** a 5-in length of the flexible beading wire, starting from the crimp bead, and **cut.**

11. **Repeat** steps 9 and 10 until you have attached eight pieces of flexible beading wire to the watch—four on each loop.

12. After deciding which side of the watch you want to work on first (it's a tom*ay*to/tom*ah*to thing), **string** a 3mm round copper bead onto one of the middle strands.

13. Using smaller beads for the ends and larger beads for the middle, **string** a random pattern of beads, spacers, caps, and so on onto the strand—tucking the tail of the wire on the crimped end inside the added beads—until you think the length is correct for your wrist size. (To check the sizing of this first strand, center the watch face on the top of your wrist and curve the beads around the joint. The beads should reach the center-point of the underside of your wrist. If the strand is too long, pluck some beads off; if it's too short, add a few.)

14. **Add** a 3mm round copper bead.

15 Using a crimp bead and your crimping pliers, **attach** the strung wire to one of the loops of the toggle clasp. (Assuming you're using a two-strand clasp, you'll want to attach the top two strands of the watch to the top loop and the bottom two to the bottom loop to prevent the strands from crossing over each other.)

16 Using your wire cutters, **cut** any excess wire from both ends of the beaded section.

17 **Repeat** steps 12–16 until you've added beads to all eight strands of beading wire and attached both ends of the toggle clasp.

Making and Attaching the Dangles

18 **String** a small turquoise bead onto a copper head pin.

19 **Form** a basic loop right above the bead.

20 **Repeat** steps 18 and 19 seven more times, for a total of eight turquoise dangles.

21 **String** a 4mm copper-colored crystal bicone onto a copper head pin and form a basic loop right above the bead.

22 **Repeat** step 21 seven more times, for a total of eight copper crystal dangles.

23 Use a 4mm jump ring to **attach** a turquoise dangle to one of the triangular jump rings attached to the watch face. The dangle should be attached to the exposed portion of the triangular jump ring—on either side of the strands of beads comprising the band.

23

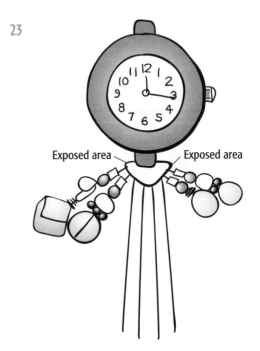

Attach the dangles to the exposed portion of the triangular jump ring, distributing them equally on the watch.

24 **Repeat** step 23 three more times on the same triangular jump ring, ending with two turquoise dangles on the exposed portion above the strands, and two in the exposed portion below.

25 Use 4mm jump rings to **attach** four copper crystal dangles to the triangular jump ring, again distributing the dangles evenly on the exposed portion of the ring.

26 Switching to the other jump ring, **repeat** steps 24–25 to attach the remaining dangles.

Variation

Ace of Face

by Kate Shoup Welsh

Even though it sort of has High School Guidance Counselor overtones, I do sometimes like wearing a timepiece on a long necklace. And if you use a watch face that has jump rings, you can easily attach some baubles to the bottom for a bit of zip. I threaded a yard-long segment of black silk cord through the top ring of a rectangular silver-ish face and, after ensuring that the necklace was adequately long for me to slip it on and off over my head, I double-knotted the ends. (To strengthen the connection, try applying a few drops of Super Glue to the knot.) I didn't bother snipping the excess cord because I thought it looked purty as it was. Next, I attached 10 jingly dangles of various types to the opposite ring.

Security Anklet

by Rachel Nelson-Smith

There's something so Mykonos, so Capri, so *Morocco* about wearing an anklet. Since Westerners face travel advisories in practically every corner of the planet, however, you might decide to settle on wearing an anklet in New Jersey or Atlanta or wherever you live. Here's one that's sure to draw attention away from your problem areas to your lovely, slender ankles.

Project Rating: Love o' Your Life

Cost: $10–$25, depending on the materials you use

Necessary Skills: Bead stitching (page 38)

Materials

- FireLine 6 lb or 8 lb test
- 10 grams 11/0 Japanese seed beads (We used matte brown AB, Toho #177F, but we'll call it "first color" in case you opt for a different set of colors.)
- 5 grams 11/0 Japanese seed beads (We used 22K gold plate, Fire Mountain Gems #4897SB, but we'll call it "second color" from here on out.)
- 2 grams 11/0 Japanese seed beads (We used opaque turquoise, Toho #55, but we'll call it "third color.")
- 20 round beads, 6mm (We used burgundy Swarovski crystal pearls #5810.)
- 19 bead chips (We chose Arizona turquoise.)
- 1 gold-filled chain, 2 in
- 2 gold-filled eye pins, 20 gauge
- 1 gold-filled head pin, 20 gauge
- 1 spring clasp
- 2 in of extender chain, the same metal tone as your clasp
- Chain nose pliers
- Round nose pliers
- Wire cutters

- 1 beading needle, #12
- Beading scissors
- Beeswax or thread conditioner
- Bead mat

Build the Anklet Body

1 **Cut** 1 yd of FireLine, wax it, and **thread** it on your needle. (You'll probably need to add more thread as you go; refer to the section "Feed Your Thread" in chapter 3 for help.)

2 **Add** a stopper bead about 6 in from the end of the FireLine.

3 **String** enough 11/0 seed beads in the first color to encircle your ankle, plus 1 in more.

4 **String** one 11/0 seed bead in the second color, followed by six more 11/0 seed beads in the first color.

5 **Pull** the needle and thread back through the single second-color bead in the opposite direction. (One end of the clasp will eventually be attached to the loop you create here.)

6 **String** eight first-color 11/0 seed beads onto the thread.

7 **Skip** over eight beads on the initial row, and then **pull** the needle through the ninth bead on that row. We'll call that bead a "center" bead.

8 **Repeat** steps 6 and 7 until you reach the end of the initial row. (Ignore any beads on the initial row that do not fit into the eight-bead pattern. You will pull these off later.)

9 After pulling the needle and thread through the last center bead in the row, string six more beads, and then pass the needle and thread back through the same center bead in the opposite direction to create the loop to which the other end of the clasp will be attached.

Fill In the "Eyeballs"

10 **String** one 11/0 seed bead of the second color, one 6mm round bead, followed by one more 11/0 seed bead of the second color. Then pass the needle through the next center bead.

11 **Repeat** step 10 until all the eye-shaped spaces are filled.

7

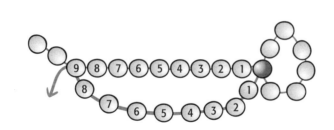

Skip the first eight beads in the initial row, and then pull the needle through the ninth.

11

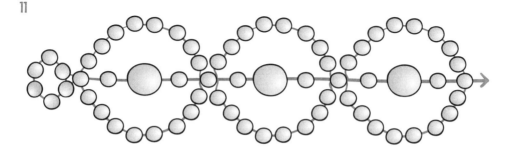

Fill in the center of each "eye" shape.

Scallop the Edges

12. Pass your needle through the six-bead loop at the end of the anklet, **pull** the needle back through the first center bead, and then **thread** through the first seven beads on the bottom edge of the body of the anklet.

13. String two 11/0 seed beads in the second color.

14. Skip the eighth bead in the first eye shape, the center bead, and the first bead in the next eye shape, and then pass the needle through beads 2–7 in the next eye shape.

15. Repeat steps 13 and 14 until you've linked all the eye shapes.

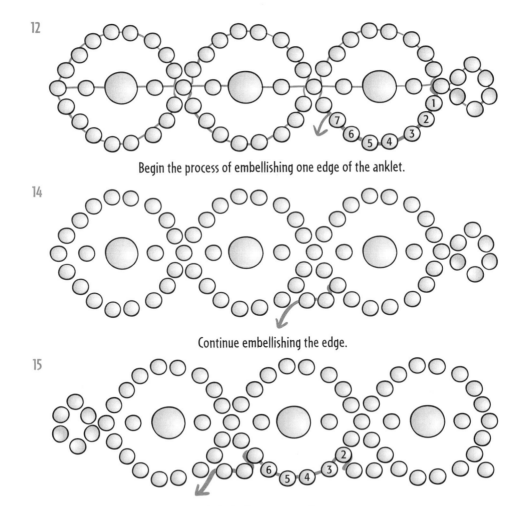

12
Begin the process of embellishing one edge of the anklet.

14
Continue embellishing the edge.

15
Link the last two eye shapes.

16 **Pull** your needle through beads 2–8 in the last eye shape, through the last center bead, around the loop at the end of the anklet, and back through the center bead a second time.

17 **Thread** through the first seven beads on the top edge of the first eye shape.

18 **Repeat** steps 13–16. When you are finished, your thread should be coming out of the last center bead, pointing toward the opposite end of the anklet.

16

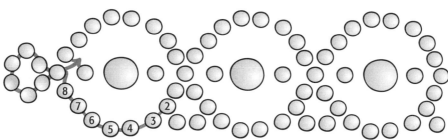

Prepare to link the top portions of the eye shapes.

17

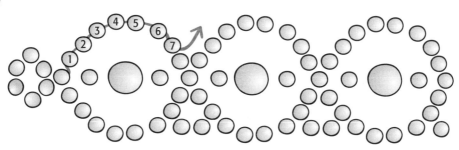

Thread through the first seven beads.

18

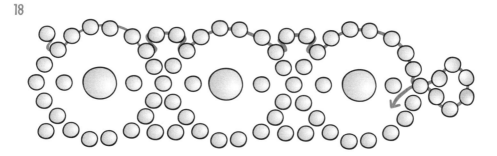

Link the eye shapes along the top and prepare to complete the bottom part.

Finish the Edges

19 **Pull** your needle and thread through the first five beads along the bottom of the eye shape.

20 **String** one 11/0 seed bead in the second color.

21 **Pass** your needle and thread through the two second-color seed beads you added on your last pass across the top edge.

22 **String** one more 11/0 seed bead in the second color.

23 **Pass** through beads 4 and 5 of the next eye shape.

24 **Repeat** steps 20–23 until you've reached the end of the anklet.

25 **Draw** the needle and thread through the last center bead, around the six-bead loop, and back through the center bead. When you are finished, your thread should be coming out of the last center button, pointing toward the opposite end of the anklet.

26 **Repeat** steps 19–25 to finish the edge along the top of the anklet.

Add Fringe

27 Now you're ready to add fringe along the bottom; you'll alternate between long and short fringe, starting with long fringe. To begin, **pass** the needle and thread through the first five first-color beads, and then through the first second-color bead that is sticking out.

23

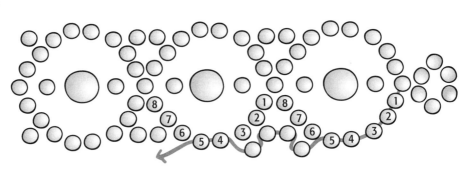

Adding the next row.

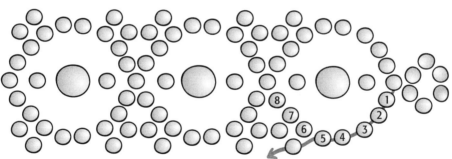

27

Prepare to add the first piece of long fringe.

28 **String** the following, in order:

- ◆ 3 first-color 11/0 seed beads
- ◆ 1, 3mm round bead
- ◆ 5 more first-color 11/0 seed beads
- ◆ 1 second-color 11/0 seed bead
- ◆ 1 bead chip
- ◆ 1 more second-color 11/0 seed bead
- ◆ 5 more first-color 11/0 seed beads

29 **Draw** the needle and thread back up the 3mm round bead, in the opposite direction from before, and then **add** three more first-color 11/0 seed beads.

30 **Pass** the needle and thread through the next second-color bead that is sticking out.

31 **String** five second-color 11/0 seed beads, and then **pull** the thread back up through beads 4 and 3.

30

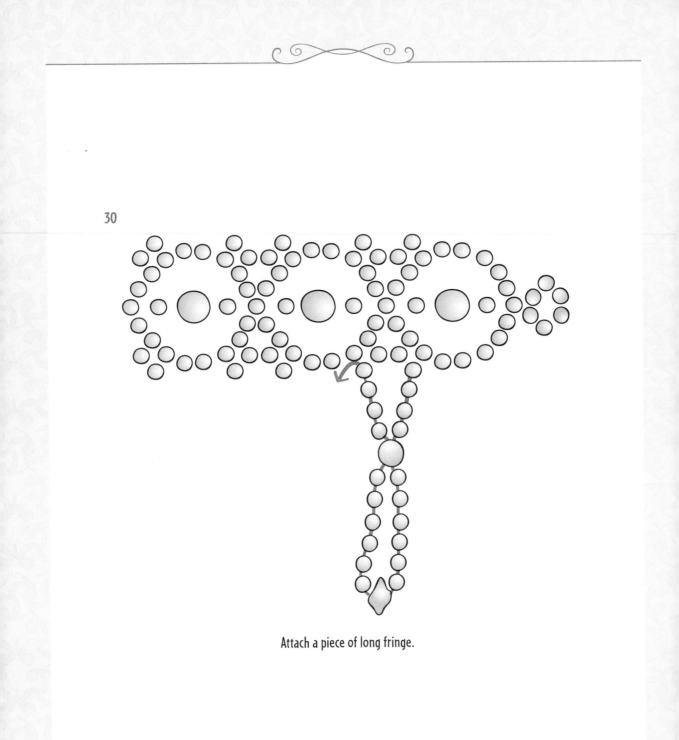

Attach a piece of long fringe.

31

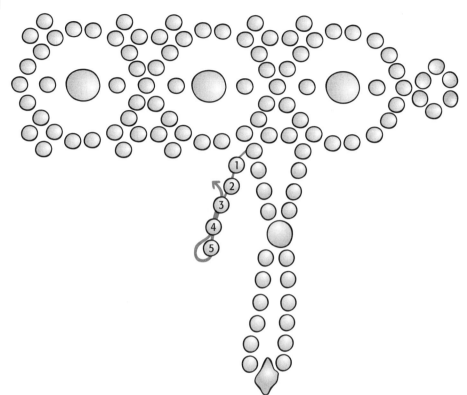

Attach a piece of short fringe.

String two more second-color 11/0 seed beads.

Pass the needle through the next second-color seed bead that is sticking out.

33

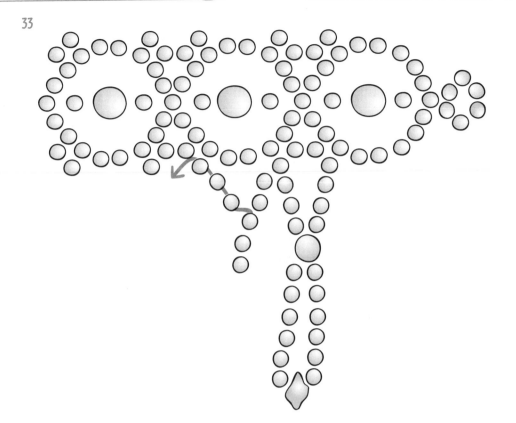

Finish the first set of fringe.

34 **Repeat** steps 28–33 until all fringe has been added. (You may end with a long fringe or a short one, depending on how long your anklet is; either way is fine.)

35 **Draw** the needle through the five remaining first-color beads on the last eye shape, through the center bead, around the loop, and back through the center bead. Your needle should be pointing toward the opposite end of the bracelet.

35

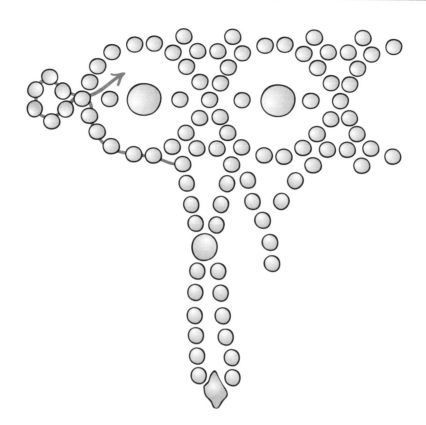

Wrap up the fringe segment.

Finish the Top

36 **Pass** the needle through the three beads that act as the "eyeball" of the first eye shape—the first second-color seed bead, the 6mm round bead, and the second second-color seed bead.

37 **String** a third-color 11/0 seed bead.

38 **Pass** through the next "eyeball."

38

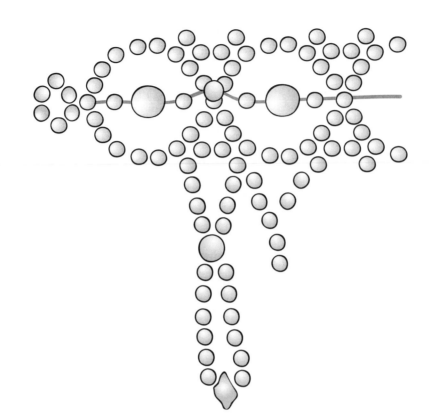

Cross your eyes!

39 **Repeat** steps 37 and 38 until the row is completed.

40 **Draw** your needle through the center bead, around the six-bead loop, through the first five first-color beads along the top of the eye shape, and then through the first second-color bead that sticks out.

40

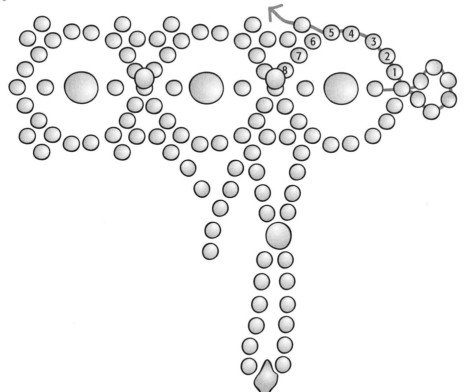

Prepare to finish the top.

41 String two third-color 11/0 seed beads.

42 Pass the needle through the next second-color bead that sticks out.

43 String *three* third-color 11/0 seed beads.

44 Pass through the next second-color seed bead that sticks out.

45 Repeat steps 41–44 until the row is complete.

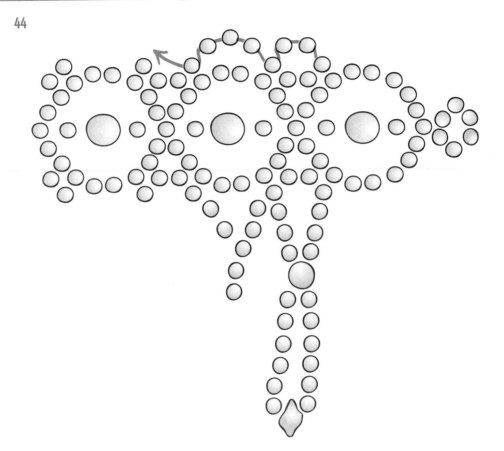

44

Add third-color beads to the top.

Tie Off

46 **Weave** the remaining thread back into beadwork and knot it.

47 **Dab** a bit of glue on the knot. (After it dries, you can snip off the excess thread.)

48 **Remove** the stopper bead and any beads that didn't fit in your original eight-bead pattern and **weave** the tail into the beadwork. **Knot** it, and then dab a bit of glue on the knot; when the glue dries, **snip** off the excess thread.

Attach the Clasp and Extender Chain

49 **Put** one 3mm round bead onto an eye pin.

50 Using pliers, **form** a simple loop at the straight end of the eye pin to create a bead link.

51 **Repeat** steps 49 and 50 to create a second bead link.

52 **Attach** one loop on either bead link to the six-bead loop on either end of the anklet.

53 **Attach** the bead link's opposite loop to the spring clasp.

54 **Repeat** steps 52 and 53, this time using the second bead link to attach the 2-in extender chain to the opposite end of the anklet.

55 **Place** a 6mm round bead on a head pin.

56 Using your pliers, **form** a simple loop, right above the bead, to create a dangle.

57 **Attach** the dangle to the end of the chain.

Variation

Choker Face

This piece is extremely easy to adapt to a lovely choker; just measure your neck in step 3 of the section "Build the Anklet Body," add 3-ish inches, and go from there. If your attention span is shorter than Gary Coleman, consider using bigger beads—I used size 6/0 seed beads rather than the 11/0s used in the anklet. I also used slightly bigger "eyeball" beads, along with two seed beads on each side, to fill the eye shape. I couldn't find any bead chips that I absolutely loved, so I substituted faceted glass drops. Finally, because I suck at measuring, my necklace wound up too short and was choking me a bit; as auto-erotic asphyxiation is not really my bag (no judgment), I extended the length by adding a few extra beaded loops to each end before attaching the clasp. (Attaching a short length of chain to one end of the choker rather than a simple jump ring would have been another good way to solve the problem.)

No Way Crochet

by Amy Swenson

If beading alone just isn't complicated enough for you, glutton for punishment that you are, you should rest easy with the knowledge that you can inflict suffering on your crafty self by combining beading and crocheting. Call it "beadcheting." Here you'll learn the ins, outs, and throughs of beadcheting a nifty bracelet.

Project Rating: Fling

Cost: $5

Necessary Skills: Wirework (page 55)

Materials

- 15 yd of 28-gauge silver wire
- 47 assorted transparent glass beads
- 1 U.S. 8/1.50mm crochet hook
- Wire cutters
- Bead mat

1 Unraveling—but not cutting—a foot or so of wire from the spool, **string** your beads onto the wire, sliding them all the way to the spool. We used the following color pattern: one clear bead, one turquoise bead, one clear bead, one lime-green bead, all of varying sizes and shapes for the most natural appearance.

2 **Create** a slip knot at the end of the wire, leaving a tail that's 6 in long, give or take. If you're a smarty-pants crochet person already, make your slip knot and skip to step 6, you showoff. Otherwise, to begin, simply **mold** the wire into a loop shape.

2

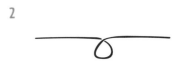

Form a loop.

3 **Fold** the portion of the wire that crosses over to form the loop downward, positioning it under the loop.

3

Fold the wire downward.

4 Using your crochet hook, **pull** the downward-pointing wire through the center of the circle.

4

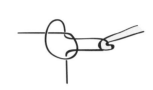

Pull the wire through the circle.

With the hook still in place, tighten the loop you created by using your fingers to **pull** the wire on both sides of the loop. (Don't go crazy with the pulling here—not too tight, but not too loose.) That's it—your slip knot is complete.

5

Baby's First Slip Knot.

Slide one bead along the wire until it is as close to the hook as possible.

Open your left palm and **drag** the wire across your palm and between your first and middle fingers.

Close your fist. The wire should be caught by your last three fingers. Then **extend** your index finger and thumb, like you're pretending to be an outlaw, or Amy Fisher with Mary Jo Buttafuoco.

Wrap the wire around the back of your index finger and then pull it toward you. Use your thumb and middle finger to hold onto the bottom of the slip knot. With your right hand, **hold** the crochet hook so the loop is about an inch from the end of the hook part, with the hook part facing away from you and pushing against the working wire (i.e., the wire that runs behind it).

9

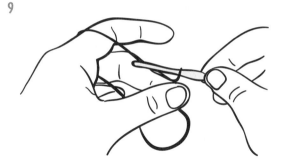

Position your hands to begin the chain stitch.

With the hook still pressed against the working wire, **rotate** the hook toward you clockwise to wrap the wire around the shaft of the hook.

10

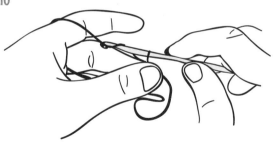

Rotate the hook to wrap the wire around the shaft.

Continue rotating the hook another quarter turn until it points down.

Pull the hook to the right to catch the wire in the hook.

Pull the hook to the right and through the loop. The bead you slid over in step 6 should also pass through the loop. You have now completed one chain stitch, and should have a new loop on the hook!

14 After pulling a little on the hook to loosen this new loop, **repeat** steps 10–13, but this time do so without adding a bead.

15 **Slide** the next bead along the wire until it is as close to the hook as possible.

16 **Complete** a chain stitch, pulling the bead through the loop.

17 **Repeat** steps 14–16, alternating between adding and not adding beads, until all 47 beads have been crocheted into the chain.

18 About 6 in beyond your last stitch, use your wire cutters to **cut** the bracelet from the spool.

19 **Wrap** the excess wire on both ends of the piece—the 6-in tail you left at the beginning, and the 6 in you just cut on the other end—around the piece several times to secure it.

20 To wear the bracelet, simply **wrap** it around your wrist three times.

Variation

Beadchet Buffet

by Amy Swenson

It goes without saying that this technique can be used to make a swell choker. To make one, we used 36 glass beads—14 square clear ones, four larger clear ones, nine lime-green ones, and nine turquoise-blue ones, again using the clear, turquoise, clear, lime color pattern. Also, rather than beadcheting a choker that had to be wrapped around our necks three times, as was the case with the bracelet, we built one that goes around only once and is secured with a toggle clasp. To accommodate the clasp, we suggest making it a point to use smaller beads on the ends of the piece to allow the toggle bar to maneuver into the toggle loop. Also, we worked in an additional five or six chain stitches at each end of the piece. To attach the clasp, simply use your round nose pliers to mold the wire at the end of the piece into a hook shape, slip the clasp into the hook, and then finish the end with a wrapped loop; repeat on the other end.

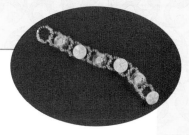

Doin' the Button

by Olga Skurat

Remember that song, "Doin' the Butt," featured in that cinematic classic *School Daze?* My guess is when they said, "When you get that notion, put your backfield in motion," the kind of notion they were referring to wasn't of the "sewing accessory" variety—i.e., buttons. Which is too bad, because I'm guessing Tanya, Theresa, Irene, Melissa, Sonya, Shirley, Tammy, and Little Keisha, all of whom reportedly have "a big ol' butt" (at least, they do in the song), would really prefer to have some big ol' buttons in order to make this bracelet. Put another way, this piece kicks *button*.

Project Rating: **Fling**

Cost: **$10**

Necessary Skills: **Bead stitching (page 38)**

Materials

- 1 yd SoftFlex or Beadalon, .014mm diameter
- 6 Swarovski crystal bicones, 4mm
- 6 vintage buttons with shanks (rather than holes), roughly ½ in in diameter
- 150 size 6/0 seed beads, give or take
- 8 size 10/0 seed beads
- 1 crimp bead
- Wire cutters
- Crimping pliers
- Bead mat

1 **String** one button onto the thread, situating it at the thread's center point.

2 **String** seven 6/0 seed beads on the thread on the left.

3 **String** seven 6/0 seed beads on the thread on the right.

4 **Add** one crystal bicone to either thread, and cross through the bicone with the other thread.

5 **Pull** each thread through the seed bead on either side of the crystal.

5

Pull the threads through the seed beads closest to the crystal.

6 **Add** six 6/0 seed beads to each thread.

7 **String** one button on either thread, cross through the button shank with the other thread, and pull each thread through the seed bead on either side of the button.

7

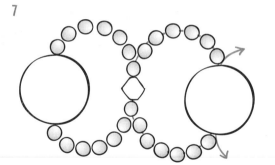

Add the next button using the same approach as with the first crystal.

8 **Add** six 6/0 seed beads to each thread.

9 **Repeat** steps 4–7 until the last crystal has been strung.

10 **Add** five 6/0 seed beads to each thread.

11 **Add** four 10/0 seed beads to each thread.

12 **Add** a crimp bead to either thread, cross through it with the other thread, and pull tight. (For a little added security, feed some of the excess thread through the adjoining beads.)

13 Use your crimping pliers to **squish** the crimp bead.

14 Use your wire cutters to **snip** any excess thread.

15 The button you added in step 1, in conjunction with the loop you created in steps 10–13, acts as a clasp; **hook** the loop over the button to close the bracelet.

Variation

Think Small

by Kate Shoup Welsh

If the vintage buttons you found dirt cheap at a flea market are smaller than the ones used here, you can easily modify this project to accommodate them. First, you'll probably want to up your numbers from six buttons to eight, and from 150ish 6/0 seed beads to 250ish smaller seed beads–say, size 10/0. Next, you'll want to play around with how many seed beads you use between the buttons and crystals–odds are the numbers cited in the steps above won't quite gel. Note that if you use smaller seed beads, you won't need to pull the thread through the seed beads on either side of the crystals and buttons after crossing through (refer to step 5), and likewise don't need to reduce the number of seed beads you string after the first crystal is added (refer to steps 2 and 3).

continued

continued

By the way, if it turns out you have buttons left over, may I humbly suggest you use one to make a ring? Poke 10 or so in of half-hard 20-gauge wire through the shank, positioning it at the wire's center point. Then wrap the wire around your ring mandrel at the correct size. Pull the right side of the wire through the button shank a second time, bend it back 180 degrees, and wrap it around the ring shank, trimming and filing excess wire as needed. Repeat with the left side of the wire, *et voilà*, a button ring for others to envy.

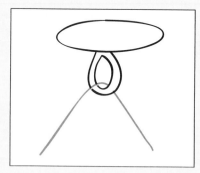

Position the button on the wire's center point.

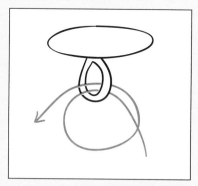

Pull the left side of the wire through the shank a second time. Repeat with the right wire.

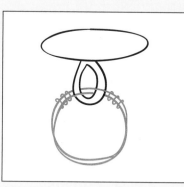

Wrap excess wire on both sides around the shanks.

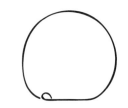

Tough Cuff

by Rachel Nelson-Smith

There's nothing cooler than a cuff. Just ask Wonder Woman. While the cuffs you'll create here won't deflect bullets—what with feminum, which is the material used to fortify Wonder Woman's cuffs, not being available to non-members of the Justice League—they *will* deflect the fashion police.

Project Rating: Fling

Cost: $25–$80, depending on whether you opt for Austrian crystals, pearls, and sterling silver or glass beads and plated wire

Necessary Skills: Wirework (page 55)

Materials

- 15 loops memory wire, bracelet width (by *width*, we mean diameter, not thickness)
- 104 first-color bicone crystals, 4mm
- 108 second-color bicone crystals, 4mm
- 60 first-color round pearl beads, 3mm
- 60 second-color round pearl beads, 3mm
- 46 first-color fire-polished Czech glass, 4mm
- 46 second-color fire-polished Czech glass, 4mm
- 46 third-color fire-polished Czech glass, 4mm
- 46 fourth-color fire-polished Czech glass, 4mm
- 46 fifth-color fire-polished Czech glass, 4mm
- 46 sixth-color fire-polished Czech glass, 4mm
- 46 seventh-color fire-polished Czech glass, 4mm
- 10 grams of 8/0 Japanese seed beads
- 6 in of 20-gauge round half-hard wire
- 18 in of 24-gauge round dead-soft wire
- 4 rondelle-shaped beads, 8mm
- 4 additional first-color bicone crystals, 4mm
- 4 round pearl beads, 3mm
- 12 in of 24-gauge round half-hard wire

- 4 sterling silver soldered 4mm, 22-gauge jump rings
- Round nose pliers
- Wire cutters
- Memory wire cutters
- Bead mat

Create the Rows of Beads for the Cuff Body

1 **Cut** 15 pieces of memory wire so each loop overlaps by ½ in.

2 **Pick up** the first loop and set the remaining loops aside.

3 Using your round-nose pliers, **form** a loop on one end of the wire, facing inward. (Don't feel all wussy if you have trouble bending the wire; it's seriously hard.) The loop should be small enough that an 8/0 Japanese seed bead won't slip through the inside of it; do yourself a favor and test it now just to make sure the size is right.

3

Form a small loop on one end of the memory wire loop.

4 Repeat step 3 on the remaining 14 memory wire loops.

5 Slide 50-ish first-color bicone crystal beads on the first loop of memory wire, until ⅓ in of the wire remains exposed. Then **curl** the end of the wire inward to form a loop—again, it should be small enough to prevent an 8/0 Japanese seed bead from slipping through the inside of the loop.

6 Repeat step 5 on a second memory wire loop with the remaining first-color bicones.

7 Repeat step 5 on a third memory wire loop with 50 or so second-color bicones.

8 Repeat step 5 on a fourth memory wire loop with the remaining second-color bicones.

9 Slide 60-ish first-color 3mm round pearl beads on a fifth memory wire loop— again, until about ⅓ in of the wire remains. As before, curl the end of the wire inward to form a small loop.

10 Repeat step 9 with 60 or so second-color round pearl beads on a sixth memory wire loop.

11 Slide 50 or so first-color 4mm fire-polished Czech glass beads on a seventh memory wire loop, again curling the end of the wire inward to form a small loop.

12 Repeat step 11 on six additional loops of memory wire with the remaining six colors of fire-polished Czech glass beads.

13 Slide some Japanese seed beads onto a 14th memory wire loop until about ⅓ in of the wire remains. As before, curl the end of the wire inward to form a small loop.

14 Repeat step 13 on one additional loop of memory wire.

Bind the Cuff Ends

15 Arrange the bracelet loops in the sequence you like best. Then, set them aside such that you can pick them up sequentially, one at a time.

16 Use round-nose pliers to form a small simple loop on one end of the 20-gauge wire; use the tip of the round-nose pliers to **center** the loop on the wire.

17 String the left end-loop of the first bracelet loop onto the 20-gauge wire.

18 String an 8/0 Japanese seed bead on the 20-gauge wire.

19 String the left end-loop of the next bracelet loop onto the 20-gauge wire.

20 String an 8/0 Japanese seed bead on the 20-gauge wire.

20

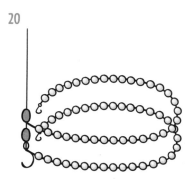

Attach your bracelet loops to a length of 20-gauge wire.

21 **Continue** stringing the bracelet loops and 8/0 Japanese seed beads on the wire until you run out of bracelet loops, but do not follow the last loop with a seed bead.

22 **Use** your wire cutters to cut the end of the wire so that only ⅜ in remains.

23 With the round-nose pliers, **curl** the remaining wire into a small simple loop.

24 **Repeat** steps 16–23, threading the wire through the right end-loops of the bracelet loops, alternating the bracelet loops with 8/0 Japanese seed beads.

Bind the Beaded Rows

25 **Cut** a 9-in piece of round, dead-soft 24-gauge wire.

26 **Bend** the wire roughly in half, with a sharp bend at the center.

27 Mentally **divide** the cuff in thirds. Then, **slip** the 24-gauge wire onto the top of the bracelet at the point that represents the division between the first third and the second third, making sure the middle point of the wire slips between two beads in the top row.

28 **Cross** the two ends of the 24-gauge wire through the space between the first and second memory wire loop and pull tight.

27

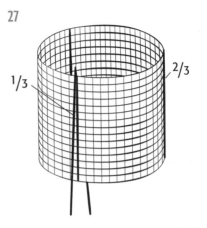

Slip the 24-gauge wire in the spot that divides the first third of the cuff from the second third. Make sure the wire settles between two beads on the top row to make it less noticeable.

28

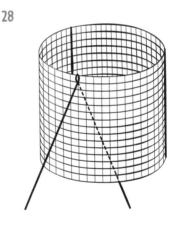

Cross both ends of the wire through the space between the first and second memory wire loop.

29 Again **cross** the ends of the wire, this time through the space between loops 2 and 3.

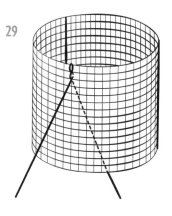

29

Cross the ends of the wire again.

30 **Continue** crossing the ends of the wire in this manner until all the memory wire loops are bound together.

31 As close to the beadwork as you can, tightly **pinch** the remaining ends of wire between the thumb and forefinger on your dominant hand, and use your other hand to **twist** the entire cuff at least five times.

32 **Cut** the twisted wire to about ⅜ in and **tuck** it back into the work.

33 **Repeat** these steps at the point in the cuff that represents the division between the second third and the third third.

Embellish the Cuff Ends

34 **Grasp** the end of the round, half-hard 24-gauge wire with the very tip of the chain nose pliers and bend it 180 degrees, creating a little hook. Then use the pliers to flatten the hook, eliminating the space in it.

35 **String** one 3mm round pearl bead, and create a wrapped loop right above the bead. **Trim** the excess wire.

36 Again with the round, half-hard 24-gauge wire, **use** your chain nose pliers to form a small hook on one end, link it to the dangle you just created, and then create another wrapped loop to secure the connection.

37 **Thread** one 8mm rondelle and one 4mm first-color bicone onto the wire, and use your chain nose pliers to form a small hook on the other end.

38 **Feed** the hook through a soldered jump ring, and then create a wrapped loop to secure the connection.

39 **Repeat** steps 34–38 to create three additional dangles on soldered jump rings.

40 **Use** chain nose pliers to open any one of the end loops in the 20-gauge wire used to bind the memory wire loops together, slip on one of the soldered jump rings that's attached to a dangle, and use the pliers to close the 20-gauge loop.

41 **Repeat** step 40 three more times on the remaining end loops to add the rest of the dangles.

Variation

Choke 'Em If You Got 'Em

by Kate Shoup Welsh

Not to sound all broken record-y, but this is another bracelet that can smoothly transition to a choker. All you need to do is use necklace-width memory wire instead of the bracelet-width variety. And of course, you'll need substantially more beads–I'd say triple what we used here, and maybe more if you're more Elizabeth Taylor circa 1981 than Elizabeth Taylor circa 1944. If you really want to get all *National Geographic* about it, add more memory wire loops than the standard 15 used on the cuff; you'll look like one of those indigenous ladies who are all about long necks.

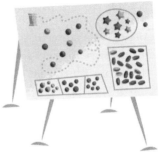

The Short and Winding Rope

by Jari Sheese

If leather is your bag—and if it is, the less said about that the better—then this is the project for you. In it, you'll use leather cord to create a fantastic bracelet with curves like Dolly Parton's.

Project Rating: Flirtation

Cost: $10

Necessary Skills: Wirework

Materials

- Sterling silver hook-and-eye clasp with crimp band (2mm leather)
- 12 in of 2mm leather cord
- 24 in of sterling silver soft round wire
- 18 Austrian bicone crystals, 6mm
- 5 Austrian bicone crystals, 4mm
- Chain nose pliers
- Round nose pliers
- Wire cutters
- Bead mat

In addition, you may opt to purchase the following:

- 5 sterling silver head pins, 24 gauge, 4 in long
- 1½-in sterling silver link chain
- 1 sterling jump ring, 4mm, 22 gauge
- Small sterling silver spacer beads

1 **Insert** one end of the leather cord into the eye end of the clasp.

2 Using chain nose pliers, **flatten** the clasp's crimp band. (Do not use a crimping tool.) Use enough pressure to secure the leather into the clasp.

3 **Tug** the leather to ensure your clasp will stay put.

4 Using your round nose pliers, **coil** one end of the sterling wire into a single loop.

5 **Feed** the leather through the loop until the coil nestles against the clasp.

Feed the leather through the coil.

6 Using your chain nose pliers, **close** the coil tightly around the leather.

7 Using your fingers, **wind** the sterling wire into four or five additional coils, pulling up tightly to ensure that each new loop sits against the previous loop.

8 **Thread** a 6mm crystal onto the wire, pushing it against the coil.

8

Add your first bead.

9 **Hold** the bead in place next to the coils on the leather and **curve** the leather over the side of the bead.

10 **Cross** the leather over the wire, and begin the coiling process by pulling the wire tightly around the leather. Coil four or five times, leaving no gaps.

10

Create a coil around the leather on the other side of the bead.

11 **Repeat** steps 8–10, curving the leather in an *S* pattern after adding each bead. (Make sure the leather is on top of the wire before you coil the wire around it.) Sixteen crystals, 6mm in size, will create a 7-in bracelet.

12 **Trim** any excess leather, leaving a small tail to fit the hook end of the clasp over.

13 **Insert** the hook end of the clasp and use your chain nose pliers to **flatten** the clasp's crimp bead.

14 *Optional:* If you'd like your bracelet to be an adjustable length, **open** the jump ring listed among the optional supplies and use it to **attach** the chain, also listed among the optional supplies, to the eye end of the clasp. **Close** the ring securely with the chain nose pliers.

15 To add some flair to the chain, **affix** a few dangles. To begin, **thread** one of the small accent sterling beads onto each of the five head pins, followed by the 4mm crystals. Then use wrapped loops to **attach** these dangles to the end of the chain, **cut** any excess with wire cutters, and **tuck** any ends down securely.

16 Put on wrist and **enjoy**! (This step is not optional.)

Variation

Twisted Sister

by Jari Sheese

Of course, you don't have to limit yourself to using crystals; just about any type of bead will do. You don't even have to use beads of a consistent size. Instead, try mixing them up a bit to create a more free-form *S* shape. Alternatively, you can dress up the design by loading it with dangles, like the ones you had the option of adding to the end of the chain in step 15. On one of our bracelets, we affixed a jump ring with dangles to each curve in the leather to add some serious sparkle.

Spiked Punch

by Tanya Tegmeyer-Rodriguez

If you're more Angelina Jolie than Jennifer Aniston, then this spiked bracelet is the project for you. The spikes convey tough, as in "Hi, I'm Lara Croft, and I'm about to kick your ass" or "Why yes, that vial around my neck *does* contain Billy Bob Thornton's blood," while the sparkles scream ladylike, as in "Nice to see you, Mr. U.N. guy."

Project Rating: Fling

Cost: $40

Necessary Skills: Bead stitching (page 38)

Materials

- 28 Swarovski crystal bicones, 6mm
- 8 grams of size 6 seed beads
- 3 grams of size 11 seed beads
- 2 grams of size 15 charlottes or other size 15 seed beads (If you like, you can substitute size 11 seed beads.)
- Lobster claw clasp
- 5 ft 6 lb FireLine (or Nymo D)
- Beeswax or thread conditioner
- Super Glue
- Fine-tipped scissors
- Size 12 sharp beading needles
- Bead mat

Construct the Base

1 **Cut** a 3-yd piece of FireLine and condition it using beeswax or another thread conditioner. (You will use more thread in the piece, but it's way easier to work with a shorter length. In fact, if 3 yd is too long for you, you can start with an even shorter piece. You can add more thread as you get further along; see the section "Feed Your Thread" in chapter 3, "Bead It," for instructions.)

2 **String** a needle onto each end of the thread.

3 You'll use a double-needle right-angle weave to stitch the base of this bracelet, as outlined in chapter 3. To begin, **string** three size 6 seed beads on either one of the needles and move them to the center of the thread.

4 **String** a size 6 bead on either one of the needles and then pass the other needle through the same bead, going in the opposite direction. Pull on both threads to tighten the stitch; the four beads should form a square.

5 **String** one size 6 seed on each needle, and move both beads down to the center of the thread.

6 **String** a size 6 bead on either one of the needles and pass the other needle through the same bead in the opposite direction. Pull on both threads to tighten the stitch.

7 **Continue** this pattern until the bracelet is long enough for your wrist. (Remember to account for the clasp—usually half an inch.)

8 When you're finished with the pattern, **weave** your needles back through all the beads to tighten the bracelet and to make it lay better.

Add the Crystal Spikes

9 **String** two size 11 seed beads on each thread.

10 On one needle, **string** a 6mm Swarovski crystal followed by a size 15 seed bead.

11 **Pull** the other needle up through the crystal and the size 15 seed bead, in the same direction as the first needle (*not in the opposite direction, as before*).

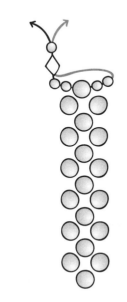

Begin adding the crystal spike.

12 **Pass** both needles back down through the crystal *only*, so the size 15 seed bead is sitting on the top of the crystal.

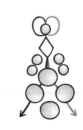

Pull the needles back through the crystal, but not the size 15 seed bead.

13 **String** two size 11 seed beads on each thread.

14 **Cross** the needles through the middle bead in the base and pull tight.

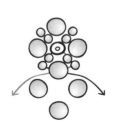

Finish adding the crystal spike.

15 **Repeat** steps 9–14 to continue adding seed beads and crystals until you have covered the entire base row. When you are finished, one thread should be coming out of each side of the last bead on the bracelet.

15

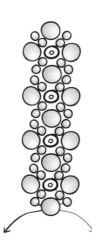

Continue adding studs until you have covered the base row.

Fill in the Gaps

16. If you look at the sides of the bracelet, you will notice gaps between the beads that run along the side of the bracelet's base. The next step is to fill each of those gaps with a size 6 seed bead. To begin, **pull** either one of your needles through the first bead on the side of the base, **string** a size 6 seed bead, and then **pull** your needle through the *next* bead on the side of the base. **Continue** in this manner until you have filled each gap on that side of the bracelet with a size 6 seed bead.

17. **Repeat** step 16 with the other thread on the other side of the bracelet.

18. **Cross** your needles through the last bead at the end of the bracelet's base.

16

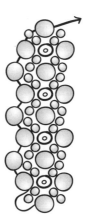

Fill in the gaps along the base row.

18

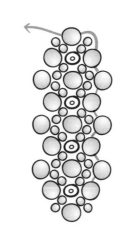

Finish filling in the gaps, and cross your needles through the last bead on the bracelet.

Attach One End of the Clasp

19 To attach the clasp, **string** three size 11 seed beads, one side of the clasp—either the lobster claw or the ring it closes on—and three more size 11 seeds onto either thread. (You'll only use one thread to attach the clasp; the other thread won't come into play.)

20 **Pull** the thread through the last bead at the end of the base of the bracelet, going in the same direction as before, and then **pull** the thread through all the beads (and the clasp) you just added.

21 **Repeat** step 20 one more time to reinforce the clasp.

21

3 times

Add one side of the clasp.

Reinforce the Bracelet

22 To make your crystals lay a bit straighter, **pull** either one of the needles up through the first two size 11 seed beads at the base of the first crystal; then **string** down through the next two size 11 beads on the same side of the bracelet.

23 **Draw** the needle through the first size 6 gap-filling seed bead on that side. (The size 6 beads that filled in the gaps will stick out a little farther than the others.)

24 **Continue** through the beads in this manner, down the rest of that side of the bracelet. When you get to the end, cross through the last bead at the end of the bracelet's base.

25 Using the other thread, **repeat** steps 22–24 on the other side of the bracelet.

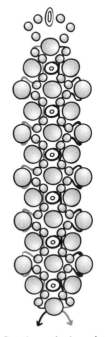

25

Reinforce the bracelet.

Wrap It Up

26 To attach the other part of the clasp, **repeat** steps 19–21 in the section "Attach One End of the Clasp" on the other end of the bracelet.

27 **Weave** the threads through a few beads in the bracelet base.

28 In a portion of the bracelet where the threads will not show (most likely somewhere on the bracelet's back side), **knot** the two threads together.

29 **Repeat** step 28 two more times.

30 **Tie** any other loose threads in the same manner. If you've wound up with a single thread by itself, **knot** it around one of the bracelet's inner threads.

31 **Dab** a drop of glue on any and all knots.

32 When the glue dries, **snip** any excess thread.

Variation

Billy Idol Called—He Wants His Bracelet Back

by Tanya Tegmeyer-Rodriguez

If the look you're going for is more tough than demure, consider widening the bracelet, à la Billy Idol circa 1985. To do so, first decide how many rows wide the bracelet should be (we opted for four), and then find a multi-strand clasp that has one fewer loop than you have rows (we picked a three-strand clasp since our bracelet was to be four rows). Next, follow the steps in the section "Construct the Base." When you get to the last square of the row, follow the steps in the section "Bead Weaver: The Right Angle Weave" in chapter 3 to add three additional rows. Then do the following:

1. **Add** spikes to the row you just completed, following the steps in the section "Add the Crystal Spikes."

2. When you finish adding spikes to the row, one thread should be coming out of each side of the last bead of the row. To begin adding spikes to the next row, you'll need to have one thread coming out of each side of the last bead on the *next* row. To get there, first **pull** the needle on the right through the bead that connects the square on the first row with the square on the second one, and the rest of the way around the first square of the second row. Next, **pull** the needle on the left through the remaining three beads of the last square of the first row a second time, and then through the top bead of the first square on the second row. (Okay, I know that's confusing as all hell, so just look at the diagram here to see what I'm talking about.) **Continue** adding spikes to the rows until you cover them all.

continued

2

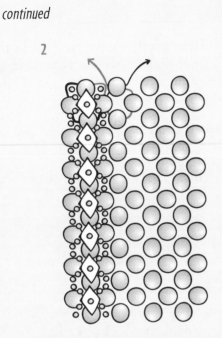

4

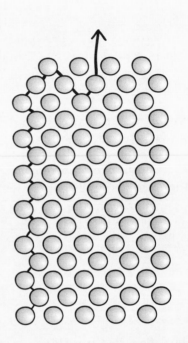

Get to the next row.

Situate the needle so you can begin adding the clasp.

3. **Follow** step 16 in the section "Fill in the Gaps" to fill in the gaps on the outer part of the row to which you just finished adding spikes.

4. Your next step is to **add** the clasp to the edge of the bracelet. First, however, you have to get your needle to the right spot. Using the same needle you used to fill the gaps, **zigzag** through the squares along the edge as shown here. (Note that we didn't show the spikes here so you'd be able to see a bit better where the thread goes.)

5. **String** three size 11 seed beads, the center loop of one side of the multi-strand clasp, and three more size 11 seed beads onto the thread. Then **pull** the needle back through the top bead in the row and around the square. To secure the clasp, repeat this step, stringing through the size 11 seed beads, through the clasp loop, and around the square. Finally, **string** through the size 11 seed beads and through the clasp loop a third time; then draw the needle downward through the top bead of the diamond.

5

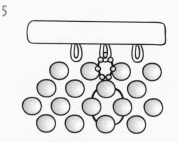

Follow this thread path three times, and then draw your needle downward through the top bead of the diamond.

6. **Weave** your way to the next connection point as shown, and **attach** the next loop of the multi-strand clasp as before. This time, however, rather than merely drawing the needle downward through the top bead of the diamond after rein-forcing the connection between the clasp and the bracelet, **thread** around the diamond one more time so that the needle is pointing upward.

6

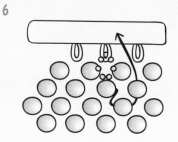

Weave to the next loop of the clasp.

7

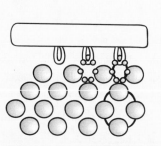

Follow this thread path three times, and then thread around the diamond one more time, stopping after the needle passes upward through the rightmost bead of the diamond.

7. **Weave** back across the bracelet to the final connection point as shown, **attach** the final loop of the clasp, and then weave through a few beads, **tie off** the thread, **dab** it with some glue. (Wait until the glue dries to snip off any excess thread.)

8

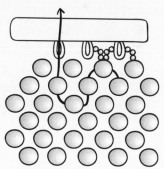

Prepare to attach the final loop.

continued

continued

8. I swear you are almost finished; you just need to **add** the clasp to the other end of the bracelet, and fill in the gaps on the other outer edge. On the side you just finished, you filled in the gaps before adding the clasp; here you'll **add** the clasp first. Repeat steps 4–7 to do so using the needle on the other end of the bracelet.

9. Now you're ready to fill in the gaps on the remaining outer edge—but you have to get your needle in the right spot first. To do so, **weave** your needle back across the edge of the bracelet as shown. Once the needle is in the right spot, fill in the gaps, **weave** through a few beads in the bracelet, **tie off** the thread, **dab** it with some glue. (Again, wait until the glue dries to snip off any excess thread.)

9

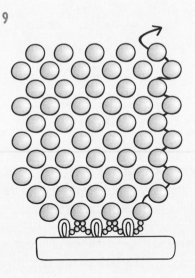

Fill in the remaining gaps, tie off your thread, and go have a beer.

Chapter Six

◆◆◆

With This Ring (and These Earrings), I Thee Thread

Hoop Therapy

Who needs group therapy? *Hoop* therapy is the way to go. You may stay crazy, but you'll look divine.

Girl with a Curl Earring

Pearl earrings? Who needs 'em when you can have a curl earring?

Swinging from the Chandeliers

Tier it up with these dazzling danglers

Bling a Ding Ring

Why should Paris Hilton have all the fun? You, too, can have baubles the size of marbles.

Nesting Instinct

Express your nest instincts with this swell ring.

Bead the Ball

Roll your own golf-ball–sized solitaire.

Catch Your Own Bouquet

Don't rough up the bridesmaid next to you in the struggle to catch the bride's bouquet! Catch your *own* with this bouquet-inspired ring.

Hoop Therapy

by Kate Shoup Welsh

Among the easiest-to-make beaded items are hoop earrings, especially if you buy little pre-fab hoops from your local bead shop. Just choose your baubles, string them on, and call it a day. (Okay, there is *one* additional step. And there are a few things you can do to make things harder if you're a purist—but still, super easy.)

Project Rating: Flirtation

Cost: $3

Necessary Skills: Wirework (page 55)

Materials

- 4 Swarovski crystal bicones, 4mm
- 4 sterling silver rounds, 6mm
- 2 lampwork rondelles, 10mm
- 1 pair 1-inch pre-made hoops (Small-gauge wire—say, 24 or 26 gauge—can also be used here; you'll need to mold it into the shape of a hoop by wrapping it around some cylindrical object that's the desired diameter. Also, steer clear of the super soft stuff; otherwise, it won't keep its shape.)
- Chain nose pliers
- Round nose pliers (if you form your own hoop out of small-gauge wire)
- Bead mat

1. **String** one 4mm crystal bicone, one sterling silver round, one 10mm rondelle, another sterling silver round, and another 4mm crystal bicone onto one hoop.

2. Using your chain nose pliers, **bend** the end of the hoop where you added the beads up 90 degrees such that it can poke through the hole on the other end of the pre-made hoop. (The portion of the wire pointing up should be relatively short.)

3. If you formed your own hoop out of small-gauge wire, you'll need to **form** a small simple loop on the other end of the hoop, through which you'll feed the upward-pointing bit in order to close the earring.

4. **Repeat** steps 1–3 to create the second earring.

Variation

Roll Your Own

by Kate Shoup Welsh

Everybody always thinks of hoops as being circular because, well, they are—in real life, anyway. But hoop earrings can be all sorts of shapes—ovals, rectangles, squares, even spirals. Also, although hoops often pass directly through one's ears, there's no law against affixing a hand-made hoop to an ear wire. We experimented with the whole hoop thing by forming some 20-gauge wire into a large spiral, pounding the crap out of it with a hammer and anvil to create a flattened effect, and then threading a few 6mm sterling silver rounds onto it. We then formed a wrapped loop at the top of the spiral and affixed it to a French ear wire.

Girl with a Curl Earring

by Charissa Brannen

If you're like me, which is to say blindingly covetous of all people with curly hair but perm-phobic, I humbly suggest the next best thing: curly *earrings*.

Project Rating: Flirtation

Cost: $8–$15, depending on the stones you choose

Necessary Skills: Wirework (page 55)

Materials

- 2 pear-shaped drop stones, 10–12mm, each with a hole pre-drilled sideways
- 2 lengths of link chain, ½ in (The weight of the chain you choose should complement your stones, without looking too heavy.)
- 2 lengths, 3 in, of half-hard 18-gauge sterling silver round wire
- 2 lengths, 2 in, of half-hard 22-gauge sterling silver round wire
- 2 lengths, 1½ in, of half-hard 22-gauge sterling silver round wire
- 2 French ear hooks
- Chain nose pliers
- Wire cutters
- Bead mat

Construct the Dangling Stone

1. **Slip** one of the 3-in lengths of 18-gauge wire through the hole in one of the stones, positioning the stone at the wire's center point.

2. While holding the stone and wire firmly in place, **bend** both ends of the wire upward, tightly around the edge of the stone, until they cross at the top.

2

Wrap the wire close to the upper half of the stone, with the free ends crossing.

3. Using your chain nose pliers, **clamp** onto one of the wires where it crosses with the other, as close to the stone as possible. Then **bend** that wire so that it appears straight up from the stone like a stem at a nice, sharp angle.

3

Bend one of the wires upward.

4. Still using your chain nose pliers, **clamp** onto the other wire—the bit you *didn't* bend—and **coil** it tightly around the stem three or four times, starting where the stem bends and moving upward.

4

Place the tightly spaced coils as close as possible to the top of the stone.

5 Using the wire cutters, **nip** the end of the wire you just coiled around the stem as close as you can, but *don't* cut the wire that comprises the stem. You'll need that for your next step!

6 **Form** a hook shape with the stem and slip one end of one of your ½-in lengths of chain onto the hook-shaped stem.

7 Use your pliers to **mold** the stem into a wrapped loop. (Make sure the ½-in length of chain doesn't slip out of the loop before you wrap it!) Note that the coils you create here will overlap the ones you made in step 4.

8 Use your wire cutters to **nip** the wrapped wire as close as you can, and then use your pliers to **flatten** any protruding edges.

8

You should now have a stone dangling from a ½-in length of chain.

9 **Repeat** steps 1–8 to create the dangling stone for the second earring.

Create the Curls

10 **Grasp** one of the 2-in lengths of 22-gauge sterling silver round wire in one hand and, with the chain nose pliers in your other hand, **clamp** onto the very end of the wire so that the pliers are perpendicular with the wire.

11 **Twist** the pliers to create a small spiral shape.

12 Now use your pliers to **grab** the other end of the wire, and **twist** in the opposite direction to create another small spiral.

12

Create an S-shaped design with spiral ends.

13 **Repeat** steps 10–12 with the 1½-in length of 22-gauge sterling silver round wire to create a second spiral *S* shape.

14 **Repeat** steps 10–13 to create the curls for the second earring, mirroring the shapes in the first earring to create a symmetrical look.

Assemble the Earring

15 **Interlock** the two spiral pieces you made for the first earring by slipping the ends over each other. This version hangs on the outer edge of the spiral, but yours can hang anywhere you'd like.

16 **Slip** the free end of one of the lengths of ½-in chain with the dangling stone onto the larger spiral piece.

17 **Slip** the loop of one of the earring hooks onto the smaller spiral piece. You now have a single completed earring.

18 **Repeat** steps 15–17 to assemble the second earring.

Variation

It Curl

by Kate Shoup Welsh

The spiral-y bits you made in the section "Create the Curls" make great connector pieces for bracelets or necklaces. Simply whip up several spirals and hook them together. If you've got some aggression to work through, consider taking a mallet to the spirals to flatten them a bit. You can even add a few beads to the spirals to add a dash of color.

Swinging from the Chandeliers

by Kate Shoup Welsh

The next time you're invited to the *Vanity Fair* Oscar party, you'll want to wear these earrings with that delicious Zac Posen loaner gown. Intricate and sparkly, they put the "hot" in "Omigod she looks so hot." Be warned, though, that you'll want to make them well before the big event, as you will almost certainly ruin your fingernails in the process. The ones we made involved three tiers of beaded dangles, but you can, of course, go longer (or shorter) if you want.

Project Rating: Love o' Your Life

Cost: $20ish, depending on the beads you choose (more if you opt for sterling silver wire and findings)

Necessary Skills: Wirework (page 55)

Materials

- 14 ft of 28-gauge silver-toned wire
- 2 bead caps that feature holes around the bottom edge (The instructions here assume your bead cap, like ours, has 9 holes. If, like Barbie, you think "math is hard," we urge you to find a cap with the same number of holes. Otherwise, you'll need to readjust the numbers of beads, lengths of wire, and such accordingly, which pretty much requires the smarts of a NASA scientist.)
- 2 crappy round beads that are small and bland enough to fit inside the bead cap without being visible (I chose 6mm clear-ish glass junkers.)
- 2 sturdy 3-in head pins
- 2 French ear wires
- 20 natural (read: globby) pearls
- 20 amber-colored faceted glass beads, 6mm
- 36 lavender faceted glass beads, 2mm
- 56 clear faceted glass beads, 4mm

- Wire cutters
- Round nose pliers
- Chain nose pliers
- Bead mat

1 **Cut** the silver wire into 54, 3-in lengths.

2 **Create** a spiral-shaped head pin with one of the lengths of wire. (For help, see the section "Go Findings Yourself" in chapter 3, "Bead It.")

3 **Repeat** step 2, 17 more times. You should wind up with 18 spiral-shaped head pins.

4 **Create** a wrapped-loop head pin with one of the lengths of wire. (For help, see the section "Go Findings Yourself" in chapter 3.)

5 **Repeat** step 4, 35 more times. You should wind up with 36 wrapped-loop head pins.

Thread one pearl onto a spiral-shaped head pin, and then create a hook shape with the wire above the bead. **Repeat** five more times, until you have six spiral-shaped headpins with one pearl each—three for each earring.

Thread one clear glass bead, one amber glass bead, and another clear glass bead onto a spiral-shaped head pin, and then create a hook shape with the wire above the beads. **Repeat** five more times, until you have six spiral-shaped head pins with this pattern—three for each earring.

Thread one lavender glass bead, one clear glass bead, and another lavender glass bead onto a spiral-shaped head pin, and then create a hook shape with the wire above the beads. **Repeat** five more times, until you have six spiral-shaped head pins with this pattern—three for each earring.

8

Create six dangles of each pattern, forming the top portion of the wire into a hook.

Thread one pearl onto a wrapped-loop head pin, and then create a hook shape with the wire above the bead. **Repeat** 17 more times, until you have 18 wrapped-loop head pins with one pearl each.

Thread one clear glass bead, one amber glass bead, and another clear glass bead onto a wrapped-loop head pin, and then create a hook shape with the wire above the beads. **Repeat** 17 more times, until you have 18 wrapped-loop head pins with this pattern.

Thread one lavender glass bead, one clear glass bead, and another lavender glass bead onto a wrapped-loop head pin, and then create a hook shape with the wire above the beads. **Repeat** 17 more times, until you have 18 wrapped-loop head pins with this pattern.

Hook a spiral-shaped headpin with a pearl bead onto the bottom of a wrapped-loop head pin with an amber bead surrounded by two clear beads. Then, **close** the hook on the spiral headpin and **form** a wrapped loop to secure the connection between the dangles.

12

Attach a spiral-shaped head pin with a pearl to a wrapped-loop head pin with two clear beads and an amber bead.

Hook the two-tiered dangle you created in step 12 to a wrapped-loop head pin with a clear bead surrounded by two lavender beads, and **form** a wrapped loop on the middle head pin to secure the connection between the dangles. I'll call this variation of three-tiered dangle "dangle one."

13

—Lavender bead combination

—Amber bead combination

—Pearl bead

Add the third tier to the dangle to create "dangle one."

14 **Repeat** steps 12 and 13 five more times. When you finish, you should have six identical versions of dangle one.

15 **Repeat** steps 12–14 six times, this time creating identical three-tiered dangles with the pearls on the top, the lavender bead combinations in the middle, and the amber bead combinations on spiral-shaped head pins on the bottom. I'll call this type of three-tiered dangle "dangle two."

15

—Pearl bead

—Lavender bead combination

—Amber bead combination

"Dangle two" has the pearl on top, the lavender bead combination in the middle, and the amber bead combination on the bottom.

16 **Repeat** steps 12–14 six times, this time creating identical three-tiered dangles with the amber bead combinations on the top, the pearls in the middle, and the lavender bead combinations on spiral-shaped head pins on the bottom. I'll call this type of dangle "dangle three."

16

—Amber bead combination

—Pearl bead

—Lavender bead combination

"Dangle three" has the amber bead combination on top, the pearl in the middle, and the lavender bead combination on the bottom.

17 **Hook** one "dangle one" to every third hole on one bead cap, forming a wrapped loop on each dangle to secure the connection. When you're finished, you should have three evenly spaced dangles attached.

17

Attach three "dangle ones" to the bead cap, spacing them evenly.

18 **Repeat** step 17 with the other bead cap, attaching three evenly spaced "dangle ones" and securing each connection with a wrapped loop.

19 **Hook** one "dangle two" to every third hole on the first bead cap, securing each connection with a wrapped loop. **Repeat** with the second bead cap.

20 **Hook** one "dangle three" to the remaining holes on the first bead cap, securing each connection with a wrapped loop. **Repeat** with the second bead cap. Both bead caps should boast nine very swing-y and sparkly dangles, creating a tassel-like effect.

21 **Thread** one crappy bead on a sturdy head pin, and thrust the head pin through one of the bead caps with dangles attached from the bottom up so that the inside of the cap rests on the bead.

22 **Add** a pearl, an amber bead, and a clear bead to the head pin, above the bead cap.

23 **Form** a wrapped loop with the remaining head pin wire and use your wire cutters to snip any excess.

24 **Repeat** steps 21–23, adding the head pin to the other bead cap.

25 **Attach** ear wires to the wrapped loops you just created to finish the job.

Variation

The Declaration of Hindi Pendants

by Kate Shoup Welsh

If you're prone to carpal tunnel syndrome, or just lack the patience to create two of the tassels required for earrings, consider half-assing it by making only one tassel and using it for a pendant. The look is remarkably exotic–sort of Vishnu-ish, I'd say–especially if you string the tassel on a long strand of beads.

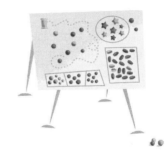

Bling a Ding Ring

by Kate Shoup Welsh

Just because you're not Paris Hilton doesn't mean you shouldn't have a *rully* big ring. And with these instructions in hand, you won't even have to be briefly engaged to a Greek playboy who favors trucker hats (but not, it seems, baths) to get it. By the way, this ring doesn't have to go on your finger; these same basic steps can be used to string a great toe ring.

Project Rating: Flirtation

Cost: Expect to spend $5—maybe more if you opt for a super bling-y focus bead

Necessary Skills: Bead stringing (page 33)

Materials

- 4mm Swarovski crystals, 8–10, depending on how meaty your finger is. (Note that you're not limited to using crystals here; spacer beads, for example, are a great option, as are simple seed beads.)
- 1 large focus bead (Mine was a kick-*ass* red faux cinnabar rectangle, about ³/₄-in across. If yours is significantly larger or smaller than this, you'll want to adjust the number of 4mm Swarovski crystals—or spacer beads or seed beads—accordingly.)
- Elastic cord (I used .7mm Stretch Magic. Whatever brand you use, the cord should be as thick as possible while still accommodating the sizes of the holes in your beads.)
- Beading scissors
- Bead mat
- *Optional:* A toothpick and a teeny dab of adhesive (I used E6000.)

1. **Cut** a 5-in length of elastic cord.

2. Beginning with the focus bead, and then adding the Swarovski crystals, **string** your beads onto the elastic cord.

3. Use an overhand knot (or two or three or four) to tightly **join** the two ends of the elastic cord.

4. Using your scissors, **trim** the ends from the knot, leaving no more than a few millimeters of cord in place.

5. **Dab** a dot of glue onto your toothpick, and then use the toothpick to swab the glue inside your focus bead.

6. **Adjust** the placement of the knot such that it is inside the focus bead.

7. **Place** the ring on your finger. Gesticulate often.

Variation

Play Wristy for Me

by Roxane Cerda

Extending your bling a ding ring into a bling a ding . . . er, *bracelet* is simple. You'll just need to stock up on some additional Swarovski crystals and consider using a larger focus bead. (Of course, you're not limited to the Swarovski crystals/focus bead format here; all types of beads, in myriad combinations, will work.) You'll also want to cut a longer strand of elastic cord–10 or 12 in should do the trick, unless you were Sylvester Stallone's wrist double in *Over the Top,* in which case you might want to go a bit longer.

Nesting Instinct

by Danielle Tooley

Once, while in the third trimester of pregnancy, with ankles the diameter of a missile silo, I experienced a profoundly powerful nesting instinct. Suddenly, it was imperative that I—or, more precisely, my husband—paint every room, reorganize every cabinet, and scrub every visible surface in the house. Frankly, it would have been a hell of a lot easier to just make this "nest" ring and leave it at that. (Not that it would have fit on my bratwurst fingers, mind you.)

Project Rating: Flirtation

Cost: $10–$15, depending on the materials you select

Necessary Skills: Wirework (page 55)

Materials

- 20-gauge sterling silver wire (dead soft) or 22-gauge gold-filled wire (dead soft)
- 26-gauge sterling silver wire (dead soft)
- 1 round or disk-shaped bead, 6–8mm
- Wire cutters
- Chain nose pliers
- Ring mandrel
- Bead mat
- *Optional:* diamond file

1 **Cut** at least 14 in (more if more "nest" is desired) of 20-gauge sterling silver wire or 22-gauge gold-filled wire, for forming the base and nest of the ring.

2 **Locate** the center of the wire, and **place** it on the desired ring size on the mandrel.

3 **Wrap** the wire around the ring mandrel three times.

4 Using the chain nose pliers, **bend** each end of the wire 90 degrees, away from the center of the ring. This will form a space in which to insert the bead.

4

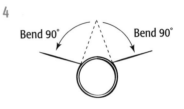

Bend both ends of the wire away from the center of the ring.

5 **Cut** 6 in of 26-gauge sterling silver wire.

6 Tightly **wrap** one end of the 26-gauge wire around one of the bent-edge wires three times.

7 **Slip** your bead onto the 26-gauge wire.

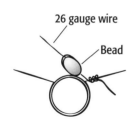

7

26 gauge wire

Bead

Wrap one end of the 26-gauge wire around one of the bent-edge wires.

8 **Wrap** the remaining length of the 26-gauge wire around the other bent-edge wire three times to secure the bead to the ring.

9 **Snip** any excess 26-gauge wire from the ends.

10 Using your fingers, **wrap** the remaining portions of the longer wires around the bead to form the "nest." Tuck the ends of the wire underneath the bead.

11 If necessary, **blunt** the sharp ends of the wire using a diamond file.

Variation

Nest Obsessed

by Kate Shoup Welsh

If you just can't get enough of this technique, double up by using it to make a set of earrings. The steps involved are similar to the ones used to make the ring; here's the low-down:

1 **Cut** two 14-in lengths of 20- or 22-gauge wire.

2 Using your round nose pliers, **create** three loops at the center point of each length of wire. The loops you create should be large enough to cradle your "egg" bead. (Incidentally, I used 8mm Swarovski crystals as my eggs.)

3 Using your chain nose pliers, **bend** both ends of one length of wire away from the loops. Instead of bending the ends to the side, however, as you did in step 4, bend the wire *forward* at a 90-degree angle. Repeat with the other length of wire. You have now created the base of both earrings.

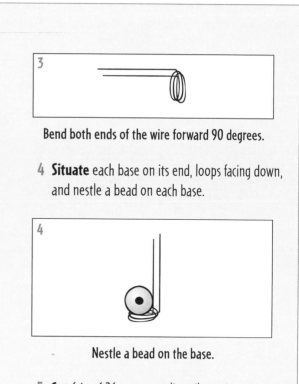

3

Bend both ends of the wire forward 90 degrees.

4 **Situate** each base on its end, loops facing down, and nestle a bead on each base.

4

Nestle a bead on the base.

5 **Cut** 6 in of 26-gauge sterling silver wire.

continued

continued

6 Tightly **wrap** one end of the 26-gauge wire around one of the base's bent-edge wires three times. Repeat for the other base.

7 **Slip** the 26-gauge wire through the bead on one base; repeat for the other base.

8 **Wrap** the remaining length of the 26-gauge wire around the other bent-edge wire three times to secure the bead to the ring. When you're finished, snip any excess 26-gauge wire from both bases.

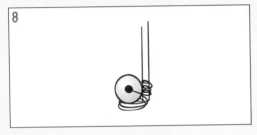

Secure the "egg."

9 Using your chain nose pliers, bend the 20- or 22-gauge wire on one base sideways at a 90-degree angle. (The bend should occur just below the bead's drill holes.) Repeat for the other base.

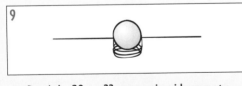

Bend the 20- or 22-gauge wire sideways at a 90-degree angle.

10 Using your fingers, **wrap** the remaining portions of the 20- or 22-gauge wire around the bead on one base to form the "nest," tucking the ends of the wire underneath the bead. Repeat for the other base.

11 If necessary, **blunt** the sharp ends of the wire using a diamond file.

12 **Cut** two 2-in lengths of 20- or 22-gauge wire.

13 Use a wrapped loop to **attach** one of the 2-in lengths of wire to one nest. Attach the remaining length of wire to the remaining nest.

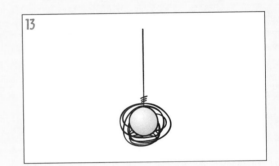

Thread one length of wire through some of the wire comprising the nest, and then form a wrapped loop to create a dangle.

14 To purty up the wires you've attached to the nests, **add** a couple beads to each one. (I used one 4mm crystal bicone and one 6mm pink crystal round on each wire.)

15 Use a wrapped loop to **attach** each embellished nest dangle to an ear wire, ensuring that the dangle and ear wire are positioned such that the nest will face forward when worn.

Bead the Ball

by Kate Shoup Welsh

For the sake of love, you've endured baseball, football, basketball, and, perhaps, a few other varieties of balls we won't mention here. Now it's time to get some balls of your own—*beaded* balls, that is. In this project you'll discover how to fashion one of these great baubles into a Regina Rich—*esque* ring.

Project Rating: Flirtation

Cost: $3

Necessary Skills: Bead stitching (page 33)

Materials

- 12 crystal rounds, 4mm (Look for beads with pretty large holes.)
- 35 size 6/0 seed beads
- Monofilament thread
- Elastic thread, .5mm width (We used Stretch Magic.)
- Super Glue
- Sharp scissors
- Bead mat

Create the Ball

1. **Cut** a 1-ft length of monofilament thread.

2. **Thread** three crystal rounds onto the thread, situating them at the center point.

3. **Add** a fourth crystal round to either thread end, and cross through it with the other thread end. This is the first "side" of the ball, which, in case you didn't notice, was created using a right-angle weave.

4. To create the second side of the ball, continue with the right-angle weave. **Thread** one crystal round onto each thread end, **add** a second crystal round to either end, and **cross through** it with the other.

5. **Repeat** step 4 one time to create the third side of the ball.

6. **Add** one crystal round to one thread end, and then **pull** that thread through the end bead on the first side of the ball.

6

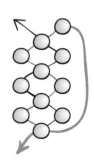

Begin the process of creating the fourth side and "closing" the ball.

7. **Add** one crystal round to the other thread and then cross that thread through the end bead on the first side of the ball.

7

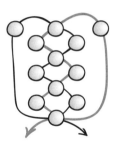

Add the last round.

8 Pull tight to form the ball, and then **tie** the two ends together in an overhand knot.

8

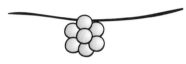

Form the ball and knot the ends of the thread.

9 Reinforce the bead ball by weaving the ends of thread through the beads, knotting as you go.

10 Dab some Super Glue on the knots.

11 After the Super Glue dries, use sharp scissors to **trim** any excess thread.

Build the Ring Band

12 Cut an 18-in length of .5mm elastic thread.

13 Draw the elastic thread through any crystal round in the bead ball, situating that round at the thread's center point.

14 String one 6/0 seed bead onto each thread end.

15 String a second 6/0 seed bead onto one of the thread ends, and then cross through the seed bead with the other end. (Again, in case you didn't notice, you're doing a right-angle weave here.)

16 Continue with your right angle weave until the ring band is just shy of being long enough to wrap around your finger.

17 After crossing the threads through a 6/0 seed bead, **add** one bead to one thread, and then draw that thread through the crystal round in the bead ball opposite the one in step 13.

17

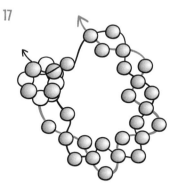

Begin attaching the band to the opposite crystal round.

18 String one seed bead onto the other thread (i.e., the end that *didn't* pass through the crystal round).

19 **Pull** tight, and **tie** the ends of the thread in a tight overhand knot.

20 **Reinforce** the band by weaving the ends through the seed beads, knotting as you go.

21 **Dab** some Super Glue on the knots.

22 After the Super Glue dries, use sharp scissors to **trim** any excess thread.

Variation

Mr. Ball Dangles

by Kate Shoup Welsh

Bead balls make great earring components. I made some swell dangle earrings using orange bead balls I'd fashioned. I began by stringing a bead that was too large to fit inside the bead ball onto a head pin. Then I added the bead ball, topping it off with a sparkly faceted glass bead. You could also use a bead ball as a pendant or focus bead, stringing it onto a necklace.

Catch Your Own Bouquet

by Arturo Rodriguez

It's a staple on every episode of "America's Funniest Home Videos": footage of crazed singletons clawing and slapping each other with the tenacity of Pro Bowl defensive backs, each girl desperate to intercept the bouquet being tossed by a smug bride—all because of a wacky superstition that says the broad who catches the stems is next in line for a ring. I say, Sisters Unite! No more dance floor skirmishes, pitting singleton against singleton! All those smug marrieds *are laughing at you!* Beat them at their own game by snaring your own bouquet *and* your own ring—all in one.

Project Rating: Fling

Cost: $20, give or take, depending on the beads you choose

Necessary Skills: Wirework (page 55)

Materials

- 10 or 12 in of half-hard 20-gauge sterling silver wire (The exact length of the wire will depend on your skill level when it comes to pulling and wrapping the wire; the more skilled you are, the less wire you'll need.)
- 1 cup bead with a hole big enough to accommodate 2 wires, 20 gauge.
- 2-in sterling silver head pins or ball pins, 14 (or more if you want your "bouquet" to be particularly full or if your cup bead is larger than normal)
- 4mm or 6mm Swarovski crystals and/or pearls, at least 14—more if you want to use multiple beads on each head pin or ball pin
- As many sterling silver spacer beads as desired
- Chain nose pliers
- Round nose pliers
- Wire cutters

- Knife (a standard-variety butter knife will do the trick)
- Ring mandrel
- Bead reamer or round needle file (to enlarge cup hole if needed)
- Bead mat

1. **Fabricate** the first "stem" of the bouquet—a dangle with one or two crystal or pearl beads and few sterling silver spacer beads on a head or ball pin. Form a wrapped loop with the wire above the beads trimming any excess.

2. **Repeat** step 1 as many times as needed to finish all the stems for the ring.

3. **Locate** the center point of the sterling silver wire, and then use the round nose pliers to **form** a loop there. Without pulling the pliers out of the first loop, **create** a second loop. You should now have two loops in the center of the wire, with two

even (or *mostly* even) segments of wire on both sides of the loops.

3

Create two loops, right next to each other.

4 Still using your round nose pliers, **grasp** the bottom portion of the loops, and use your fingertip to **bend** one of the lengths of wire down 90 degrees.

4

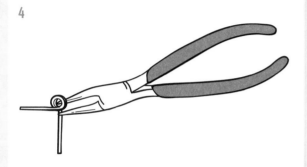

Bend one end of the wire down.

5 **Bend** the length of wire on the other side of the loops down 90 degrees.

5

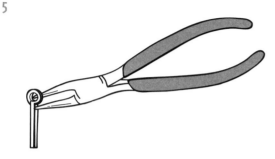

Bend the other end of the wire down.

6 Using a dull knife, **separate** the two loops to create room to feed the bead stems onto the wire.

7 **Feed** the bead stems onto the wire, nudging them onto the loops. For best results, alternate wires, adding one stem to the right, one to the left, one to the right, and so on. That way, you wind up with an equal number of stems on each loop, which creates a more balanced look.

7

Feed the bead stems onto the wire, alternating sides, and nudge them onto the loops.

8 After you've jimmied all the stems onto the loops, **pinch** the ends of the wire tips together and **push** them through the hole in the cup bead so that the stems nestle into the cup. (If the bouquet looks a bit sparse, now's the time to add more dangles; simply hook some additional dangles onto the wire loops before wrapping the ends of the dangles.)

8

Pinch the ends of the wire tips together and push them through the hole in the cup bead.

Pull the ends of the wire in opposite directions, as tightly as you can.

Place the bead cup on your ring mandrel at the desired size, and then **bend** the ends of the wire around the mandrel one time, in opposite directions. When you finish, you'll have two large loops under the bead cup, forming the shank of your ring, with the ends of the wire pointing in opposite directions.

10

Pull the ends of the wire around the mandrel to form the ring's shank.

Use the thumb and index finger of your left hand to hold the ring tight on the mandrel, with the handle of the mandrel toward your body. Then, **loop** the wire on the right counter-clockwise around the bottom of the bead cup one time, and **pull** tight to create a neck.

Repeat step 11 using the other wire. The bead cup with bead stems should now be firmly attached to the shank of the ring.

11

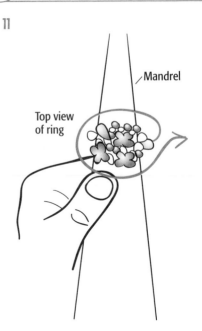

Mandrel

Top view of ring

Circle the bottom of the bead cup with the wire on the right, and pull tight.

12

Circle the other wire around the bottom of the bead cup to complete the neck.

13 **Remove** the ring from the mandrel. Then, **bend** the wire on the right into the interior of the ring, wrap it around the two wires that comprise the shank of the ring, and pull tight (use the chain nose pliers to make this a bit easier). Repeat at least twice.

13

Wrap the wire on the right around the shank of the ring.

14 **Repeat** step 13 with the wire on the left.

15 At this point, you probably have somewhere between 2 and 2½ in of wire on each side of the ring. If you like, you can finish your project by simply using your wire cutters to **snip** the wires on each side of the ring flush and then use the chain nose pliers to tuck the ends under. If you want a bit of extra polish, however, you can form a spiral with the remaining wire on each side. Your best bet is to bend the wire downward and then form the spiral; when the spiral closes in on the body of the ring, flip the spiral over the top of the shank. (For a refresher on creating spirals, revisit the section "Go Findings Yourself in chapter 3, "Bead It.")

15

Begin forming the spiral by creating a tiny half circle at the end of the wire.

Variation

Nice Stems

by Kate Shoup Welsh

You can easily create swell earrings by making a few minor adjustments to prevent the "bouquets" from weighing down your earlobes. First, rather than create 14 bead stems for each earring, create 14 stems *total*—seven for each earring. Next, instead of using a cup bead, try using bead cones; that way, your bouquets won't look pitifully spare. Then, instead of forming a ring shank out of the wires as you did in step 10 above, form two small loops; these comprise the loop you will use to attach the bouquet to an ear wire. You can then secure the loops by wrapping wire ends around the bottom of the bead cone, as you did steps 11 and 12 with the bead cup. Instead of wrapping once, however, wrap two or three times. (Use your round nose pliers, rather than the ring mandrel, to hold the loop in place as you wrap.) Finally, snip the ends to finish the job. Repeat these steps to make the second earring.

Chapter Seven

◆◆◆

Ornamentation Nation

Hair Tactics

These beaded combs and barrettes give new meaning to "hair style."

Wifebeader

Rescue this icon of abuse with some purty beads.

Zip It

Accent your fave hoodie with a sizzling-hot zip pull.

Cuff Drops

Here it is: a beaded goodie for *him*.

Handbagger Helper

Stop the insanity! Make your keys easy to find with this gorgeous keychain.

Call Me!

Texting? *So* last week. Spread *your* message with this nifty cell-phone strap.

Girls Gone Bridaled

Every girl needs a tiara. Here's one you can make with your own two hands.

Hair Tactics

by Kate Shoup Welsh

You don't have to be Bo Derek or Rick James to wear beads in your hair. Embellishing a hair comb or barrette with some gorgeous baubles can be a great way to make every day a good hair day.

Project Rating: **Flirtation**

Cost: **$3**

Necessary Skills: **Bead stitching (page 38)**

Material

- 1 undecorated auto-lock barrette or hair comb
- Several flat, square-shaped beads with holes drilled through the sides as opposed to the faces, wide enough to span the width of the barrette or comb
- Monofilament thread
- E6000 glue
- Sharp scissors
- Super Glue
- Bead mat

1 Using your sharp scissors, **cut** an 18-in length of monofilament thread.

2 **Feed** the monofilament through a single bead, situating the bead at the center point of the thread.

3 **Cross** both ends of the thread through a second bead, pulling tight but ensuring that the beads line up end to end rather than face to face.

3

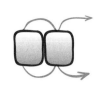

Line up the beads end to end.

4 **Repeat** step 3, crossing through additional beads, lining them up end to end, until the segment of connected beads roughly equals the length of the barrette or hair comb. (If the beads and barrette or comb don't match up exactly, err on the side of too long.) When you finish, thread should emerge from both sides of the last bead you added.

5 If you've opted to decorate a barrette rather than a comb, take a moment to **pop off** any removable pieces of the closure. You'll reattach them later.

6 **Slather** some E-6000 glue on the portion of the comb or barrette where the beads will be attached.

7 **Center** the segment of beads lengthwise on the comb or barrette, and **press** the beads into the glue.

8 **Wrap** the thread that emerges from the last bead you added around the comb or barrette to the underside, **pull** tight, and **knot** it. (If you're working with a comb, make sure your thread doesn't catch any of the comb's teeth as you wrap it; you'll want to slide the thread between the teeth closest to the hole in the bead from which the thread emerges.)

9 **Cross** the ends of the thread back through the same bead, **wrap** it around the barrette or comb again, **pull** it tight, and **knot** it on the back side a second time to secure the connection.

10 **Cross** the thread through the next bead in the row, **wrap** it around the barrette or comb, **pull** it tight, and **knot** it on the back side.

11 **Cross** the ends of the thread back through the same bead, **wrap** it around the barrette or comb again, **pull** it tight, and **knot** it on the back side a second time to secure the connection.

12 **Repeat** steps 10 and 11 until you've secured each bead onto the barrette or comb. (If your thread begins to run out, tie it off on the under side of the barrette or comb, pull a new thread through the last bead you secured such that the bead is located in the thread's center point, and continue on like *nothing ever happened*.)

13 After you've tied the second knot for the last bead, **dab** some Super Glue onto each knot in the piece.

14 Give the Super Glue a chance to dry, and then use your scissors to carefully **trim** any excess monofilament thread.

Variation

Snobby Pins

by Kate Shoup Welsh

As a person who sucks at math, I frequently overestimate the number of beads needed for a project, meaning I have some left over. Fortunately, if you've wound up with a few extra spare squares or other flat-ish beads, you can use them to make some *rully* cute bobby pins. Instead of using plain-old, drugstore-variety bobby pins, visit your local craft store to purchase special crafty bobby pins with little metal "pads" on the top (these can often be found in the Bridal section). Then, squeeze a bit of E6000 glue on the pad and press a bead onto the glue. Rest the bobby pin bead-down on a flat surface, propping the other end up with a pencil or what have you, until it dries.

Wifebeader

by Rianne Keedy

Okay, I realize the title of this project—a reference to the slang term used to refer to a tank-top style undershirt worn as an outer layer, derived from the stereotype that these shirts are worn in this manner predominantly by men who beat their wives—is unbelievably offensive, and has almost certainly alienated every card-carrying member of the National Organization for Women, an organization I deeply respect and support. But Wikipedia (O bastion of truth and accuracy) said that although some people find the term "extremely offensive," others find it "harmless or even humorous," and I confess that I am among the latter. It goes without saying that I absolutely do not endorse spousal abuse. Seriously, I swear, I'm a nice person. I hope you'll forgive me.

Project Rating: Fling
Cost: $11
Necessary Skills: Sewing

Materials

- An appropriately sized tank top
- .5mm thread (We used clear Stretch Magic.)
- 300 (give or take) size 10/0 or 11/0 seed beads in the colors of your choice
- A thin needle (We used one from an assortment pack purchased at the grocery store. Sadly, the size 10 hard bead needles purchased specifically for this project featured eyes that were too narrow to accommodate the cord used to string the beads. *Caveat emptor.*)
- Sharp scissors
- Bead mat

1 **Decide** on the bead design and colors you want to use for this project, and then **pick** through your beads to find the necessary colors. We opted for a simple design—dots of color sewn along the stitch line of the binding around the tank's neck hole.

2 **Cut** an 18- to 24-in length of cord from the spool. (Try to angle the scissors when cutting the cord; a slant on the end of the cord can make all the difference in the world when it comes to threading the needle.)

3 **Thread** the needle and **tie** a few knots at the tail end of the cord.

4 You can start stitching wherever you like, but we began at the left shoulder seam, stitching around the front of the shirt before continuing on to the back. In any case, wherever you want to begin, **poke** your threaded needle through the shirt from the inside out and **pull** until the knots you created in the thread act as a stopper.

5 **String** one seed bead on the thread and then poke the needle back through the shirt from the outside in. Pull the thread firmly, keeping it taut—but not *so* taut that the fabric bunches when released.

4

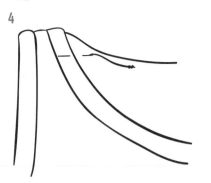

Poke the needle from the inside of the shirt out.

5

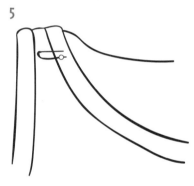

Add your first bead.

6 **Poke** the needle through the shirt from the inside out—but do so between the points where the needle went through in steps 4 and 5.

7 **String** a seed bead on the thread and then **poke** the needle back through the shirt from the outside in. The needle should enter the fabric at a point beyond the stitch you made in step 5. (For those of you who, like me, took Construction and Manufacturing instead of Home Ec during middle school, this is called a *back stitch*.)

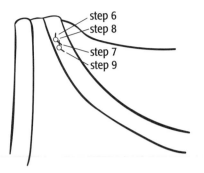

Use a back stitch to continue adding beads.

8 **Continue** using a back stitch to add beads to the binding of the tank top. We bunched our beads closer together on the front of the tank, spreading them out across the back.

9 If you run out of thread, **tie** a secure knot on the underside of the fabric, **sew** through a few more beads on the top side of the fabric, and then **pass** the thread back down through the fabric and **knot** it again. Finally, **snip** any excess thread.

10 **Begin** a new thread by knotting the tail of the thread as in step 3 and sewing through a few of the existing beads before adding new ones.

11 When you finish adding beads, **tie** off your thread in the manner described in step 9, snipping any excess.

Variation

Belt One Out

by Kate Shoup Welsh

Stitching beads onto ribbon is a great way to make a fancy-schmancy belt. You can sew on any design you like, and either affix a D-ring or some other type of buckle to one end or tie it in a fancy bow anytime you want to wear it. Either way, you'll want to finish the ends of the ribbon to prevent fraying; your best bet is to "hem" the tips. Simply tuck the raw end under and, using thread that's similar in color to the ribbon, stitch it into place. Finally, use an iron to press the seam. (This technique works well with velvet and grosgrain ribbon. I'm guessing, though, that you'll want to steer clear of sheer ribbon or else the ends will continue to look messy in spite of your hard work.) If you really want to go crazy, you could stitch a few seed beads on the end to up the "Dude, That's Cool" factor.

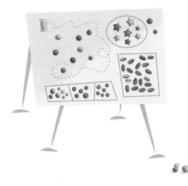

Zip It

by Rachel Nelson-Smith

Those YKK zipper people might have cornered the market on fasteners, but they haven't cornered the market on fabulousness. Wearing zipper pulls is a great way to prettify even the most mundane garments (think: hoodies). Adding a little jangle to your slobwear is a great way to fake your way to glamour.

Project Rating: Flirtation

Cost: $5 (give or take, depending on what type of beads you choose)

Necessary Skills: Wirework (page 55)

Materials

- 1 lanyard hook clasp, ³/₄ in
- 1 sturdy head pin or eye pin of any style, decorative or plain (If you want to add a second dangle to the bottom of your pull, as we did for one of ours, up your number of pins to 2, making sure at least 1 of them is an eye pin.)
- 1 large bead, such as a Venetian glass bead or some other nifty bauble (Make sure it's not *so* heavy that it'll pull your zipper down against your will! Alternatively, you can choose 2 or 3 smaller beads—one of our pulls featured a 10mm Swarovski crystal pearl, a 6mm vintage German glass bead, and a 4mm Swarovski round crystal bead.)
- 1 or 2 accent beads (For example, we used 2 small Swarovski bicones on 2 of our pulls to add some sparkle. Our other 2 pulls, however, used no accent beads. All this is to say, don't fear the Jewelry Gestapo if you opt out here.)
- 2 sterling silver spacer beads (Again, not a requirement—we used spacer beads on only 2 of our pulls.)

- Round nose pliers
- Chain nose pliers
- Wire cutters
- Bead mat

1 **Place** your beads on your head pin or eye pin in the desired order, creating a wrapped loop on the top. (If you want a second dangle to hang from this first dangle, you'll want to use an eye pin in this step, with the eye on the bottom.)

2 Optionally, **create** a second, smaller dangle, placing one or two small beads on a pin and forming a wrapped loop on the top.

3 If you opted to create a second dangle, **attach** it to the first, larger dangle by using your chain nose pliers to open the eye at the bottom of the larger dangle, slipping the smaller dangle onto the loop, and closing the eye.

4 **Slip** the lanyard hook clasp through the wrapped loop at the top of the larger dangle.

5 **Attach** the pull to the zipper on your plush Juicy hoodie.

Variation

Identify Yourself!

If you have one of those jobs where you have to wear your ID badge or security clearance card around–like, say, at the CIA–you're familiar with the vexing problem of wearing a lanyard without looking like a basketball referee. Solution? Attach one of these nifty pulls alongside your badges. Okay, so it probably won't boost your security clearance, but at least it'll relieve your *in*security about your appearance!

Cuff Drops

by Kate Shoup Welsh

Inevitably there will come a time when you'll need to devise some wallet-friendly gift for a person with a Y chromosome, and odds are your boyfriend/spouse/gay best friend won't be interested in the kick-ass bracelets you made for all your girlfriends' birthdays. (Well, maybe your gay best friend would be, but you get my point.) Fortunately, the cuff links featured in this project fit the bill—they're cheap, they're easy, and they look great. Kind of like you.

Project Rating: Flirtation

Cost: $5—a tad more if you use sterling silver toggle bars

Necessary Skills: Wirework (page 55)

Materials

- ◆ 2 sturdy 3-in head pins (We opted for ones that had a tastefully embellished end.)
- ◆ 2 matching rondelle-ish beads that are larger than the buttonholes (that's butt*on*holes, thank you very much) found on shirt cuffs
- ◆ 2 matching accent beads
- ◆ The bar ends of 2 toggle clasps (The ones we chose weren't terribly long—just long enough to not slip through the buttonhole when engaged.)
- ◆ Chain nose pliers
- ◆ Round nose pliers
- ◆ Wire cutters
- ◆ Bead mat

1 **Slide** one accent bead and one focus bead onto a head pin.

2 **Form** a loop with the stem on the head pin, attaching the toggle bar to the loop in the process. Make sure the loop you create is far enough away from the beads

that the bar end of the toggle has enough room to wiggle up against the stem of the head pin.

3 **Wrap** the excess wire around the stem of the head pin, all the way to the beads. That'll help keep the beads in their place.

3

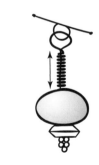

Put some space between the loop and the beads.

4 **Repeat** steps 1–3 to create the second cuff link.

Variation

Poet Lariat

by Kate Shoup Welsh

So the burning question here is, "What the hell do you do with the toggle loops that no longer have corresponding bars?" Easy—use them on lariats. We attached one to the end of a 30-in length of beading wire and then loaded the wire up with beads. We pulled the opposite end of the lariat through the toggle loop and then added a decorative dangle to that end. (Because our lariat was long enough that we'd be able to slip it on and off over our heads, we had the added flexibility of being able to add beads to the dangle that were larger than the hole on our toggle loop.)

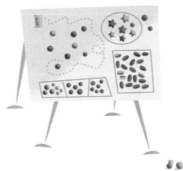

Handbagger Helper

by Sonya Rhiver

If you're anything like me, and God help you if you are, hunting for your keys is a daily ritual. Making a honking beaded key ring might be just the thing to help you keep track of them. As for limiting the number of keys on the ring so no one assumes you're the janitor, you're on your own. (Not that there's anything wrong with being a janitor, of course. I mean, seriously, maintenance is a noble job. But you know what I'm saying. Janitors *do* have a lot of keys.)

Project Rating: Flirtation
Cost: $5–$10, depending on the beads you select
Necessary Skills: Wirework (page 55)

Materials

- ♦ 5-in silver-coated base-metal sturdy head pin
- ♦ Key ring
- ♦ 5 lampwork beads (We chose a "garden party" theme, but feel free to deviate.)
- ♦ 1 glass cane bead
- ♦ 4 sterling silver spacer beads (Ours are different sizes and types, but you can be all anal-retentive about it and streamline yours if you want.)
- ♦ 1 Swarovski crystal rondelle, and a large-ish Swarovski accent bead
- ♦ 1 charm
- ♦ 1 jump ring or split ring
- ♦ Wire cutters
- ♦ Chain nose pliers
- ♦ Round nose pliers
- ♦ Split ring pliers (if you opt for a split ring over a jump ring)
- ♦ Bead mat

1 **Arrange** your beads on your design board or some other skid-proof surface until you're keen on your design.

2 **Thread** your beads onto the head pin in the desired order.

3 **Create** a loop at the top of the head pin, but don't close it quite yet.

4 **Hook** the head pin onto the key ring.

4

Hook the head pin onto the key ring.

5 Close the loop at the top of the head pin to secure it to the key ring, wrapping the remaining wire around the pin.

6 Trim any excess wire.

7 Attach the charm to the loop at the top of the head pin using either a jump ring or a split ring. (If you opt for a split ring, use your split ring pliers; it's *waaaaay* easier.)

Variation

What a Charmer

by Sonya Rhiver

Why should your car's ignition or the lock on your apartment be the only things that get a gander at your fabulous key ring? Consider making a similar bag charm to dangle from your purse strap. Not only will this maximize the impact of your fabulous *faux* Louis Vuitton, it may even help you fight crime—as in, "Stop that man! He's stolen my purse! It's the one with the fruit-inspired bag charm!" To do so, simply follow the steps above, but opt for a clippie thing, like the ones used to attach your dog's leash to her collar, instead of a key ring. A hardware store may be your best bet for finding a clippie (actually, the technical term is "swivel," but I just don't feel like that has as good a ring to it) that's large enough.

Call Me!

by Rachel Nelson-Smith

This neat-o keen cell-phone strap is a great way to convey what you're all about; simply spell out your message using letter beads. We opted for "MAD SASSY," naturally. If you'd prefer a different message, I suggest you avoid choosing the longest word in the English language—which, incidentally, not counting technical words like *pneumonoultramicroscopicsilicovolcanoconiosis*, referring to a lung disease, is *floccinaucinihilipilification*, defined as "the act of estimating something as worthless"—unless you want to sling your cell phone over your shoulder instead of toting it around on your dainty wrist. (You'll probably want to make sure your phone features a loop to accommodate a strap before you dive into this project; predictably, because I am frequently foiled, my phone does not.)

Project Rating: Flirtation

Cost: $6

Necessary Skills: Bead stringing (page 33) and wirework (page 55)

Materials

- 6 crystal or glass beads, 4–6mm (Ours were fuchsia.)
- White glass letter beads to spell out your message
- 1 head pin, 20-gauge, for each letter bead and for each crystal or glass bead
- 1 jump ring, 4mm, for each letter bead and for each crystal or glass bead
- 2 ft of 1.5mm waxed and braided cotton (If you prefer, you can use 1–2mm leather or satin cord.)
- 1 large coiled end crimp
- 1 cell phone strap
- Chain nose pliers
- Round nose pliers
- Wire cutters
- Bead mat

1 **Place** any bead onto a head pin and **form** a basic loop on the stem of the head pin, using your wire cutters to **trim** the excess.

2 **Repeat** step 1 for the remaining beads.

3 **Attach** any of the bead dangles to a 4mm jump ring.

4 **Repeat** step 3 for all the remaining bead dangles.

5 With the dangles constructed, you're ready to shift your attention to the strap. To begin, **tie** an overhand knot about 4 in from one end of the cord.

6 On the longer part of the cord (that is, *not* on the 4 in between the end of the cord and the knot), **string** the jump ring attached to the dangle containing the first letter of your message (in our case, "M").

7 **Tie** a knot very close to the first knot, but with the dangle in between the two.

8 **String** the jump ring attached to the dangle containing the next letter of your message, following up with another knot.

9 **String** the remaining letter dangles required to spell out your first word, adding a knot after each dangle.

10 After you've added the first word in its entirety, **string** two crystal or glass bead dangles.

11 **Tie** a knot after the second dangle.

12 **Repeat** steps 6–9 as many times as necessary to spell out any remaining words in your message, adding two crystal or glass bead dangles between each word.

13 When you're finished adding your words, determine how long the cord should be, and **cut** it accordingly. (You'll want the cord to be long enough to slip easily over your hand onto your wrist, but not so long that you'll accidentally fling your cell phone across the room each time you tell that funny story about your dad driving your mom's Ford Bronco into a pond, which requires lots of gesticulation.)

14 **String** the remaining crystal or glass bead dangles on each end of the cord, distributing them evenly.

15 **Pinch** both ends of the cord together and insert them into the barrel end of the crimp (that is, the end without the loop).

16 Using your chain nose pliers, **squish** the last coil of the end crimp to attach the crimp to the cord.

17 **Attach** the cell phone strap onto the loop on the other end of the end crimp.

18 **Loop** the cell phone strap onto your phone.

Variation

Eat It and Die

If you work somewhere with a communal fridge, and if your colleagues are forever pilfering snacks from your stash, may I suggest attaching a similar strap to your lunchbox? Suggested message: "EAT IT AND DIE."

Girls Gone Bridaled

by Rachel Nelson-Smith

Now that you're all grown up, it's time to trade one type of headgear—that torture apparatus your orthodontist made you wear—for another: a tiara. It won't straighten your teeth, but it will convey your fabulousness.

Project Rating: Love o' Your Life
Cost: $65 (less if you go for less-expensive materials)
Necessary Skills: Wirework (page 55)

Materials

- 85 Swarovski crystal bicones, 4mm, in crystal AB
- 10g of size 11/0 Japanese seed beads in ceylon silver-lined (AB finish is good too.)
- 60 Swarovski crystal pearls, 3mm, in white
- 50 pearlized glass drops, 5mm
- 2 ft of 16-gauge dead soft sterling silver round wire
- 36 ft of 26-gauge dead soft sterling silver round wire
- Chain nose pliers
- Round nose pliers
- Wire cutters
- Bead mat

Create the Tiara Body

1 **Cut** a 24-in length of 16-gauge sterling silver wire.

2 **Cut** a 6-in length of 26-gauge wire.

3 Using your chain nose pliers, **grip** the last ¼ in of one end of the 16-gauge wire and **bend** it up 90 degrees.

4 **Repeat** step 3 at the other end of the 16-gauge wire. Both ends should bend in the same direction—up.

5 **Bring** the wire ends together, holding them so they overlap about ¾ in.

6 Using the 6-in length of 26-gauge wire, tightly **bind** the overlapped wires together. The binding should cover no more than ¼ in of the 16-gauge wires.

6

Bind the overlapped wires together.

7 Using your wire cutters, **trim** the excess 26-gauge wire.

8 Using the tips of the chain nose pliers, **pinch** the two ends of the 26-gauge wire into the binding.

9 **Pull** the outermost parts of the 16-gauge wire in opposite directions to

sandwich the binding between the two 90-degree bends.

9

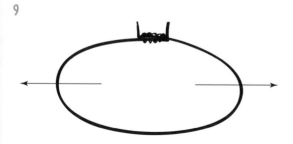

Pull the wires in opposite directions.

With the tips of your chain nose pliers, **grip** the ¼-in end of one of the bent parts of the 16-gauge wire and curl it inward to form a loop. Repeat with the other ¼-in end of bent wire.

10

Curl the ends of the wire inward.

Keeping the bound wire at the center, **bend** the circle of 16-gauge wire in half so that the opposing halves of wire run alongside each other, about ¼–½ in apart.

11

Bend the circle of 16-gauge wire in half.

With your fingers, **adjust** the wires so that they run parallel-ish. (I say "ish" because the center portions of the wire should be slightly farther apart than the ends.)

Place the deep part of your round nose pliers in the crux of wire on one side of the tiara and use your fingers to **pinch** the wire around the pliers to create a large loop. (You'll use this loop to attach the tiara to your hair with a hair pin.) When you're finished, use your fingers to again make the remaining portion of the wires run parallel-ish, keeping the loop intact.

13

Form a loop on one end of the tiara.

Repeat step 13 on the other end of the tiara.

Cover the Front of the Tiara

Cut a 3-ft length of 26-gauge wire.

Line up ½ in of one end of the 26-gauge wire alongside the pinched 16-gauge wire (refer to step 13). Then, form a right angle with the 26-gauge wire and tightly **wind** it around the ½ in of wire you just lined up. **Wrap** the wire several times, until it is secure when you pull on it.

String one 11/0 seed bead onto the 26-gauge wire, and **wrap** the wire once around the top wire of the body of the tiara from front to back. The seed bead should be on the side of the tiara facing you.

17

Add a seed bead, and then wrap the 26-gauge wire around the top wire comprising the tiara's body from front to back.

18 Pull the wire upward to tighten it.

19 To secure the wire, **pull** it downward along the backside of the tiara, **wrap** it around the bottom of the tiara from back to front, and **pull** it back upward.

19

Wrap the 26-gauge wire around the bottom of the tiara from back to front.

20 Repeat steps 17–19 once.

21 String two 11/0 seed beads onto the 26-gauge wire and **secure** the wire as before.

22 Repeat step 21 once.

23 String one 4mm Swarovski bicone onto the 26-gauge wire and **secure** the wire.

24 As the space between the parallel-ish top and bottom wires increases, so, too, will the number of beads used to fill the space between them. To that end, **string** three 11/0 seed beads on the 26-gauge wire and **secure** the wire.

25 Repeat steps 23 and 24 once.

26 String one 4mm Swarovski bicone on the 26-gauge wire and **secure** the wire.

27 String four 11/0 seed beads and **secure** the wire.

28 String one 11/0 seed bead, one 4mm bicone, and one more 11/0 seed bead, and **secure** the wire.

29 Repeat steps 27 and 28 six times.

30 String five 11/0 seed beads and **secure** the wire.

31 String two 11/0 seed beads, one 4mm bicone, and one more 11/0 seed bead, and **secure** the wire.

32 Repeat steps 30 and 31 six times.

33 String six 11/0 seed beads and **secure** the wire.

34 String two 11/0 seed beads, one 4mm bicone, and two more 11/0 seed beads, and **secure** the wire.

35 Repeat steps 33 and 34 10 times.

36 Repeat step 33 once. This will ensure that both sides of the tiara mirror each other.

37 Because the space between the top and bottom wires comprising the body of the tiara is decreasing, so, too, will the number of beads used to fill the space between them. **String** two 11/0 seed beads, one 4mm bicone, and one 11/0 seed bead, and **secure** the wire.

38 String five 11/0 seed beads and **secure** the wire.

39 Repeat steps 37 and 38 six times.

40 String one 11/0 seed bead, one 4mm bicone, and one 11/0 seed bead, and **secure** the wire.

41 String four 11/0 seed beads and **secure** the wire.

42 Repeat steps 40 and 41 six times.

43 String one 4mm bicone and **secure** the wire.

44 String three 11/0 seed beads and **secure** the wire.

45 Repeat steps 43 and 44 once.

46 String one 4mm bicone and **secure** the wire.

47 String two 11/0 seed beads and **secure** the wire.

48 Repeat step 47 once.

49 String one 11/0 seed bead and **secure** the wire.

50 Repeat step 49 once.

51 Finish off the 26-gauge wire by wrapping it tightly around the pinched wire next to the loop you created in step 14. **Wrap** the wire several times, until it is secure when you pull on it.

Running on Empty

If you employ a technique in which a smaller-gauge wire is used to embellish a larger-gauge wire, as is the case here, odds are you'll run out of the smaller-gauge wire sometime along the way. Don't freak out—finishing a wire and adding a new one is simple. Here's what you do:

1. When your smaller-gauge wire has been whittled down to about 4 in, **wrap** the remaining wire tail around a small area of work. In this project, we recommend wrapping around an area of 16-gauge wire. Wherever you wrap, make sure to wrap at least three times around, or until the wire is secure when pulled.
2. **Cut** any excess wire off as closely as possible.
3. **Cut** a 3-ft length of 26-gauge wire.
4. **Wrap** the new length tightly around an area near the spot where the previous wire was wrapped off. Be sure to wrap at least three times around, or until the wire is secure when pulled.
5. **Work** the wire to the point where you left off and continue from there.

Add the Twisted Branches

52 **Cut** a 3-ft piece of 26-gauge wire and **wrap** the end of it tightly around the top wire at the tiara's middle point.

53 Use your chain nose pliers or your thumb to **bend** the wire at a 90-degree angle about 1 in from the wire's base.

54 **Slide** any of your remaining beads—a 4mm crystal bicone, a 3mm crystal pearl, a pearlized drop, or even two or three seed beads—onto the wire until it hits the bend. This will be your first branch.

55 **Double** the wire back to snuggle up against the bead you just added, crossing the existing portion of the branch's "trunk."

55

Begin adding the branches.

56 Using your nondominant hand, **pinch** the wires just below the bead.

57 **Pinch** the bead with your dominant hand and **twist** away from you several times.

58 **Separate** the wires about ⅓ in from the base of the twisted branch and **bend** the excess wire at a 90-degree angle.

59 **Slide** a bead onto the wire until it hits the bend.

60 As before, **double** the wire back to snuggle up against the bead you just added, again crossing the trunk.

61 **Pinch** the crossed wires with your nondominant hand.

62 **Pinch** the bead you just added with your dominant hand and **twist** away from you until the branch is twisted all the way to the base.

63 If desired, **add** a few more branches to this trunk. Some of our trunks feature three, four, and even five branches.

64 When you finish adding branches to this trunk, use your dominant hand to **twist** the entire trunk all the way to the tiara base.

65 **Wrap** the 26-gauge wire once around the 16-gauge wire and **weave** to the next point to add another branch—about ⅛ in.

66 **Continue** working down the length of the tiara, adding twisted branches with beads.

67 About halfway to the end, **begin** shortening the branches, possibly adding fewer beads. **Continue** making the branches shorter and shorter until you reach the end.

68 **Finish** the wire by wrapping it tightly several times around the base of the tiara and closely trimming any excess.

69 **Repeat** steps 52–68 on the other half of the tiara, beginning in the middle and working your way out.

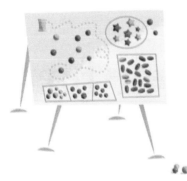

Variation

Scepter Sold Separately

In the event a pre-teen covets your tiara, gently pry it out of her tiny, grubby hands and promise to make her one of her own. Instead of using chi-chi sterling-silver wire, opt for the el-cheapo variety, and track down some colorful beads in lieu of the sedate palette used here. The result: a crown fit for any princess—royal or no.

Chapter **Eight**

◆◆◆

Gifts and Flair for Your Pied a Terre

Know Your Place
Claim the best spot at the table with these ace place markers.

Tipple Rings
Even the tipsiest girl will remember which glass is hers with the help of these wine stem markers.

Hit the Bottle
Finally! An outlet for all the buttons, beads, and other doodads squirreled away over the years.

Serviette Yourself
These napkin rings add a certain *je ne sais quoi* to any table.

Tacky Tacky
Gussy up your bulletin board with these sweet beaded tacks.

Glass Ceiling Fan Pull
Be your own biggest fan with these beaded fan pulls.

The Collar Purple
This kick-ass collar will ensure your Fido evades the fashion police's K-9 unit.

Gentle Beader
Mark your spot with this beautiful beaded bookmark.

Know Your Place

by Tracy Gritter

If you've ever invited people you envy to a dinner party, you know the importance of setting a table that is both beautiful *and* reflective of your own fabulous personality. That means carefully conveying your insouciance by perfectly mismatching your excruciatingly expensive tableware, glassware, flatware, and linens ("What, those old things?"), and demonstrating your artistic cleverness with some fabulous handmade place-card holders.

Project Rating: Flirtation

Cost: $1 per place-card holder

Necessary Skills: Wirework (page 55)

Materials

- ♦ 15 in of 16- or 18-gauge craft wire in the metal tone of your choosing (We went with silver.)
- ♦ A few medium-sized beads with large holes (It's fielder's choice on colors and styles here, but in case you're interested, we used three nonmatching glass beads with one large silver-toned spacer.)
- ♦ Chain nose pliers
- ♦ Wire cutters
- ♦ Bead mat

1 Using your pliers, **twirl** one end of the wire to form a small loop.

2 Still working with the same end of wire, **form** a heart-ish shape; it should be large enough to serve as the base for the place-card holder. When you are finished, the wire should bisect the "heart" vertically, with the long end of the wire tucked under the base.

2

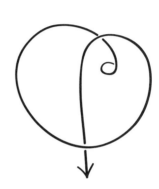

Form the base of the place-card holder.

3 **Bend** the long end of the wire up 90 degrees and add your first bead or two.

4 About 1½ in from the base, **form** a loop that's 1 in in diameter, give or take.

5 **Add** two more beads—one on the upper part of the loop you just formed, and one on the lower.

5

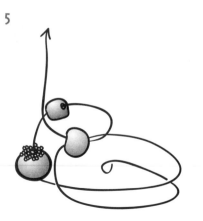

Begin constructing the body of the place-card holder.

6 **Create** another, more oblong loop that intersects with the one you formed in step 4. Tuck the wire comprising the new loop behind the one you already made.

7 Roughly 2 in above the oblong loop, **bend** the wire down and to the right, forming a 135-ish degree angle.

8 Beginning about 1½ in from the bend you just created, **form** a spiral with the remaining wire.

9 **Slot** a business card–sized place card horizontally into the oblong loop you created in step 6.

10 **Repeat** steps 1–9 to create as many place-card holders as necessary.

11 **Set** the table, placing the wealthiest, best-looking, most charming man next to you.

8

Finish constructing your piece.

Variation

If a Picture Is Worth a Thousand Words, How Much for a Frame?

This place-card holder also makes a swell picture frame. For one, unlike those frames that make you wedge your photo into a metal spiral, this frame allows you to simply rest the photo in the oblong loop. Second, the back rest you created in step 6 supports the photo from behind, preventing it from drooping. All this is to say that if you don't want to muss up that 4 × 6 snap of you and Matthew McConaughey, this is the frame for you.

Tipple Rings

by Kate Shoup Welsh

Remembering your own name—let alone whose glass of Riunite is whose—is no small feat when you and your girlfriends are on your fourth bottle of the night. That's why tipple rings (more boringly referred to as *wine stem markers*) are a requirement for any sloppy evening in.

Project Rating: Flirtation

Cost: Expect to spend $5–$10, depending on your choice of beads

Necessary Skills: Wirework (page 55)

Materials

- A total of about 25 to 40 small seed beads
- 6 unique charms
- 12 in of memory wire ($\frac{1}{2}$-in ring size)
- Memory wire cutters
- 12 memory wire end caps
- Super Glue
- Bead mat or a bead board

1 Cut the memory wire into six pieces, with each piece just over one coil in size.

2 Lay out your beads. Using a bead board, a bead mat, or any other surface that will ensure that your beads don't roll right off your work surface, decide which beads and charms will go on which tipple ring. Depending on their size, the number of beads per ring may vary. Don't worry too much about placement; most of the people who use your tipple rings will be too drunk to notice or care if the charm isn't centered just so.

3 Dab a drop of Super Glue inside of one memory wire end cap.

4 Insert one end of one memory wire coil into the memory wire end cap's glue-filled hole and hold them together until the glue dries. (Try not to glue your fingers to the ring. Or, if you're really smart, you might use latex gloves.)

5 Repeat steps 3 and 4 until all six of your tipple rings have one end cap glued on one end.

6 String the beads and charms onto each tipple ring in the order you established in step 2.

7 Repeat steps 3 and 4 to attach memory wire end caps to the other end of each tipple ring.

8 Snap the tipple rings onto the stems of your wine glasses, and party like you're still underage.

Variation

What's the Stitch?

by Kate Shoup Welsh

For all you knitters out there, these tipple rings can easily be adapted for use as stitch markers—enabling you to funnel the $3 you'd normally spend to buy a stitch marker into your wine fund. Just omit the charm and, rather than using memory wire end caps, use chain nose pliers to fold the ends of each ring onto itself.

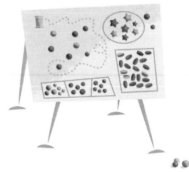

Hit the Bottle

by Barbara Walling

You already separate your plastic milk jugs from your well-read copies of *People* magazine. You even compost your dog's "deposits" into fertilizer for your herb garden. You're a *recycler*. But while recycling is unquestionably noble, it isn't always all that fun—until now. This project enables you to put the 11 wine bottles you emptied last week (no judgment) to good—and beautiful—use. Moreover, you can recycle all that crazy stuff your Great Aunt Ida hoarded because she grew up during the Depression and consequently refused to throw anything away, *ever*, like old buttons, junk jewelry, tassels, and other odds and ends—plus beads, of course. When you finish, use your bottle as a vase or just plunk it in front of a window and let it look purty.

Project Rating: **Fling**

Cost: **$5**

Necessary Skills: **Wirework (page 55)**

Materials

- A glass bottle, be it one that formerly contained wine, Snapple, Mad Dog 20/20–whatever
- 18 ft of 19-gauge wire (Go for the steel or copper wire found at your local hardware store–the kind that costs, like, $3 for 100 ft.)
- 36 ft of 28-gauge wire (Again, opt for wire available at any hardware store.)
- An assortment of beads, buttons, junk jewelry, tassels, and other odds and ends (We like to match the colors of these doodads to the color of the bottle, but it's not like anyone will shoot you if you don't.)
- Several head pins, which you'll use to create dangles (The exact number depends on how elaborate you want your piece to be.)
- Chain nose pliers
- Round nose pliers
- Wire cutters

- A dowel rod or other cylindrical object for curling the wire (The end of a broom handle does the trick.)
- Bead mat

1 **Cut** three or four 1-yd lengths of 19-gauge wire.

2 **Twist** the lengths of the cut 19-gauge wire tightly around the neck of the bottle, at the top. The remaining wires should be 18–24 in long.

3 **Mold** the ends of the wire into spirals, corkscrews, or some other interesting shape.

4 **Create** several dangles out of the head-pins and beads, but create a hook, rather than a wrapped loop, at the top. Go ahead. We'll wait.

5 **Cut** three or four 2-yd segments of 28-gauge wire. (The number of segments you cut here should match the number of segments you added to the bottle in step 2.)

6 **Wrap** one end of one length of 28-gauge wire around the base of one of the 19-gauge lengths you added in step 2 to attach it. (By "base," I mean the part of the wire that's closest to the neck of the bottle.)

7 **Continue** wrapping the 28-gauge wire around the 19-gauge wire, moving up the length of it, but space out each rotation. As you wrap, **attach** your dangles, buttons, and other one-offs by slipping them onto the 28-gauge wire and then wrapping that wire around the 19-gauge wire. Space your odds and ends one-ish or two-ish in apart.

8 When you reach the spiral or corkscrew at the end of the 19-gauge wire, **wrap** the 28-gauge wire around the 19-gauge wire several times to finish it off.

9 Using your wire cutters, **trim** any excess 28-gauge wire.

10 **Repeat** steps 6–9, wrapping 28-gauge wire around and adding baubles to the remaining 19-gauge lengths.

11 **Wrap** one of the decorated 19-gauge wires around your dowel rod, broom handle, or other cylindrical object, just like you would if you were using a curling iron to coax your hair into banana curls, *à la* Nellie Oleson on *Little House on the Prairie.*

12 **Repeat** step 11 on the remaining 19-gauge wires.

13 If you like, **stretch** out the curled wires a bit, and **twist** them in any direction to spiff up your design.

Variation

Pop Your Cork

by Barbara Walling

If you used a wine bottle in this project, consider gussying up the cork while you're at it. To do so, poke anywhere from one to three lengths of 19-gauge wire, each length measuring two-ish feet, through the cork's top. As with the bottle, bend the ends of the 19-gauge wire in the cork into a spiral; use 28-gauge wire to attach several dangles, buttons, and such; and curl the wire with a dowel rod or other cylindrical object. Wedge the embellished cork into the mouth of your decorated bottle to add a bit of extra sparkle; or anytime you pop open a nice Chianti, keep it fresh by using the cork as a stopper.

Serviette Yourself

by Kate Shoup Welsh

Gorgeous napkin rings are a boon to any table, but who wants to shell out $36 for a set of six? Here's a quick, easy way to make beautiful beaded rings to suit any table for a *song*. You may even be able to use some of the loose beads in your collection, driving the price down farther yet.

Project Rating: Flirtation

Cost: $2

Necessary Skills: Wirework (page 55)

Materials

- Assorted glass beads (It's fielder's choice on colors and styles here.)
- Bracelet-width memory wire
- Memory wire cutters
- Chain nose pliers
- Bead mat

1 Using your special memory wire cutters, **cut** a coil of wire that overlaps itself at least by half. (Ours overlapped a few times for added opulence.)

2 Using your chain nose pliers, **curl** one end of the memory wire into a simple loop.

3 If you want to be all persnickety about things, take a moment to **lay out** your beads in the desired order.

4 **String** your beads onto the wire, either in an established order or randomly.

5 **Curl** the other end of the memory wire into a loop.

6 **Repeat** steps 1–5 to create however many napkin rings you want.

Variation

Wrist Me, You Fool

Once your napkin is in your lap, why not spiral that fabulous napkin ring around your dainty wrist?

Tacky Tacky

by Denise Town

Look, your bulletin board is precious. Not only is it displayed front and center in your office for all to see, but it showcases your favorite photographs, all the best *New Yorker* cartoons, that postcard your best friend sent from Nepal, plus the digits of that guy you met at the coffee shop. Given the importance of these items in your life, shouldn't they be displayed with a bit more flair? Enter these fabulous pushpins.

Project Rating: Flirtation

Cost: $1

Necessary Skills: Bead stringing (page 33)

Materials

- ♦ Several beads with small holes (It's fielder's choice on colors and styles here.)
- ♦ Straight pins with colorful balls on top (the kind you use when sewing)
- ♦ Ear wire safety sleeves (those rubber doodads you slide on ear wires so your earrings don't fall out)
- ♦ Bead mat

1 **Add** beads to a straight pin, ending with the smallest bead. (Be sure to leave plenty of pin to stick into your bulletin board.)

2 **Slide** an ear wire safety sleeve onto the pin. *Voilà!* Instant bulletin-board chic.

3 **Repeat** until you create enough push-pins to tack up all your favorite things.

Variation

Stick It To Me

by Kate Shoup Welsh

Why should your bulletin board have all the fun? You can use this same technique to create stickpins or hatpins. Just get your hands on a stickpin or hatpin finding (they look just like headpins except the tips are *wicked* sharp; make sure you also get the little stopper jobby that goes on the pointy end), pile on a few beads, and add the ear wire safety sleeve to hold the beads in place.

Glass Ceiling
Fan Pull

by Tracy Gritter

There's nothing more annoying than being too short to turn on your own freaking ceiling fan without using a trampoline or hiring a male cheerleader to lift you up. For those of us who do not meet the height requirements for playing professional basketball or striding the cat-walk in a lovely Badgley Mischka gown, I bring you this ceiling fan pull.

Project Rating: Flirtation
Cost: $5–$10
Necessary Skills: Wirework (page 55)

Materials

- 8–10 in. half-hard 18-gauge base metal wire
- 12–24 in of ball chain (Opt for ball chain that has a fairly substantial heft so that if Kermit the Frog gets tangled up in your fan, the way he always did on *The Muppets,* the pull won't break.)
- 5 large beads with big holes (Oddly, these can be hard to find. If your bead store doesn't have what you're looking for, visit your local big box craft store and look for one of those bargain tubs of beads.)
- 1 standard ball chain connector
- 1 "Type A" ball chain coupling
- Chain nose pliers
- Wire cutter
- Bead mat

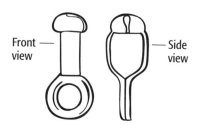

Front view — Side view

"Type A" ball chain coupling, available at most hardware stores or at www.ballchain.com.

1 **Cut** the ball chain to the desired length.

2 **Attach** the ball chain connector to one end of the ball chain.

2

Attach the standard connector to one end of the chain.

3 **Attach** the Type A ball chain coupling to the other end of the ball chain, crimping it if necessary to secure the connection. Then set the ball chain aside.

3

Attach the Type A coupling.

4 Using your pliers, **form** a spiral on one end of the 18-gauge wire.

5 **Thread** the beads onto the wire, in whatever order you like.

6 Use your pliers to **form** a hook directly above the topmost bead, and then feed the hook through the ring in the Type A coupling. Create a wrapped loop to secure the connection.

6

Attach the beaded dangle to the ball chain.

7 If you have rather a lot of wire left, you can **wrap** it around the topmost bead for decoration; then snip any excess wire.

7

Wrap the remaining wire around the topmost bead.

8 Use the ball chain connector to **attach** the new, longer pull to the existing ball chain on your ceiling fan.

Variation

Kick Ball Chain

by Kate Shoup Welsh

Ball chain makes for great jewelry, too. I like to string a single, large, brightly colored resin bead on a short necklace. If you're looking for something a little more upscale, try using sterling silver ball chain with an actual spring clasp soldered on in lieu of the little connector piece; you can find chains of varying lengths online. If you go this route, you'll probably need to use pliers to flatten the jump ring that attaches to the spring clasp in order to string the bead; once the bead is on, simply use your pliers to fiddle with the ring until it's roughly a circle again.

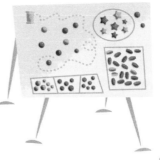

The Collar Purple

by Rianne Keedy

They say that people's pets resemble their owners. For example, just as Paris Hilton is bony and somewhat hairless, so, too, is her pet Chihuahua, Tinkerbell. Likewise, my pet resembles me, except that rather than being zaftig, insecure, and overly loud, as I am, she is a sucker for jewelry—like this fabulous beaded collar.

Project Rating: Fling

Cost: $6

Necessary Skills: Sewing

Materials

- An appropriately sized nylon collar (We used a 14-in to 20-in adjustable Hartz Living nylon dog collar, 3/4-in wide.)
- .5mm-diameter bead and jewelry cord (We used Stretch Magic but monofilament would also work well.)
- Size 11 seed beads in several colors (You'll need roughly 8 beads per flower–2 green ones for the leaves, 1 yellow one for the center, and 5 of any color for the petals. Try holding beads against the collar to make sure the beads don't clash with or disappear into the collar.)
- Sharp scissors
- A needle that's strong enough to slide through the tough nylon collar but thin enough to pass through a bead opening when threaded with the cord (We used a needle from one of those plastic disks that holds an assortment of sizes.)
- Bead mat

1 **Adjust** and size the collar to fit its recipient's neck before proceeding. (Presumably this recipient will be of the canine or feline species as opposed to, say, of the genus dominatrix. Or not.) This part is important because it determines the working area of the adjustable collar—you don't want to invest time and effort sewing beads to parts of the collar that will be obscured when the collar is sized correctly.

1

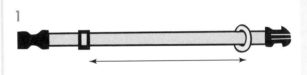

The working area.

2 Angling the scissors to create a slant on the end of the thread, **cut** a 12-in length of it from the spool and tie a couple of knots in the end to act as stoppers. (If the cord is too long, it will twist all over itself, which will be both annoying and time-consuming to untangle. On the other hand, the cord *does* need to be long enough to sew through the collar a few times even after being knotted on one end. So trust me on this—12 in is the way to go.)

3 **Thread** the needle on the cord. (Here's where you should thank me for mentioning that "angling the scissors to create a

slant on the end of the cord" bit because it makes threading the needle *way* easier.)

4 Starting 1 in or so away from the edge of the working area (I'm talking length-wise here, not widthwise), **push** the threaded needle up through the back of the collar to its front. Pull the cord through firmly, but without pulling the knotted end through the collar.

5 **Slide** the bead that will be the center of the first flower down the needle and cord until it rests on the collar, and then **push** the needle back through the collar, close to where the needle first came up. Again, pull the cord firmly, making sure there are no twists and that the bead is held securely in place against the collar. The center of the first flower is now set.

6 For the flower petals, **sew** five or six beads around the center bead, again making sure the cord is pulled tight with each stitch. (Be aware that attaching the flower-petal bead horizontally or vertically in relation to the center bead changes the appearance of the flower-petal bead. There's no right or wrong way, but if one way makes a more pleasant-looking flower, make an effort to consistently sew on the beads that way.)

7 For the leaves, **sew** one or two green beads off one side of the flower, and one or two green beads off the other side of the flower, again making sure the cord doesn't twist or knot as it's pulled through. The collar shown has multiple beads on the sides of each flower, making more of a vine than leaves.

8 After attaching the last bead and with the cord and needle coming out of the backside of the collar, **tie** a few knots in the cord as close to the collar as possible. (It never hurts to once more send the needle up through the collar and back down, and again knot it several times close to the collar.)

7

Use one or two green beads for leaves; three or four green beads can represent vines or stems.

9 **Cut** the cord close to the knot.

10 **Repeat** this process for each flower, spacing them evenly along the working area of the collar.

Gentle Beader

by Rachel Nelson-Smith

Gentle beader, you can't bead every minute of the day. You'll obviously need to make time to enjoy your favorite chick lit. But you can incorporate your love of beading into your reading by stringing this beaded bookmark. It's as easy—and as easy on the eyes—as Colin Farrell!

Project Rating: Fling

Cost: $4–$18, depending on whether you opt for sterling silver wire and findings or silver-plated, and whether you go with Swarovski crystals or faceted glass beads

Necessary Skills: Wirework (page 55) and bead stringing (page 33)

Materials

- 26 glass or plastic flower-shaped beads in a variety of cheery colors, drilled through the center of the bead's face as opposed to through its sides (Ours were slightly cupped.)
- 6 glass or plastic green leaf beads, drilled from top to bottom
- 37 fuchsia crystal rounds, 3mm (We used Swarovskis.)
- 34 silver jump rings, 4mm (We used sterling silver.)
- 26 silver daisy-shaped spacer beads, 4mm (We used sterling silver.)
- 1 ft of .014 or .015 flexible beading wire (Beadalon or SoftFlex works well.)
- 2 medium-sized tube-shaped crimp beads
- 4 soldered 7mm silver jump rings (i.e., jump rings that can't be opened)
- 32 1-in head pins
- 6 in 20-gauge silver-tone wire
- 90 light-green iridescent 11/0 seed beads

- 20 dark-green iridescent 11/0 seed beads
- Chain nose pliers
- Round nose pliers
- Wire cutters
- Crimping pliers
- Bead mat

Make the Body of the Bookmark

1 **Cut** 1 ft of flexible beading wire.

2 Using a crimp bead and your crimping pliers, **attach** a 7mm soldered jump ring to the end of the flexible beading wire.

3 **String** one 3mm fuchsia crystal round, one dark-green seed bead, and nine light-green seed beads.

4 **String** one dark-green seed bead, one 3mm fuchsia crystal round, and one more dark-green seed bead.

5 **String** nine light-green seed beads.

6 **Repeat** steps 4 and 5 eight more times.

7 **String** one dark-green seed bead and one 3mm fuchsia crystal round.

8 **Repeat** step 2 to attach a 7mm soldered silver jump ring onto the remaining end.

9 **Cut off** the excess wire as close to the fuchsia crystal as possible.

Construct the Flower and Leaf Dangles

10 **String** a 3mm crystal, a silver daisy spacer, and a flower bead onto a head pin, such that the open part of the flower is pointing toward the end of the head pin.

11 **Form** a simple loop out of the wire right above the flower bead, and then use your wire cutters to snip the excess wire.

String the flower-shaped bead with its open end facing the "pin" on the wire, and then form a simple loop at the top of the dangle.

12 **Repeat** steps 10–11, continuing to make flower dangles until you run out of flower beads. (You should have 26 flower dangles when you finish.)

13 **String** a leaf bead onto a head pin and form a simple loop.

14 **Repeat** step 13, continuing to make leaf dangles until you run out of beads. (You should have six leaf dangles when you finish.)

Assemble the Dangles

15 **Form** a simple loop on one end of the 6-in length of 20-gauge silver wire. The loop should be just large enough to hook around your 7mm soldered jump ring, plus a little extra room for movement.

16 **String** a 3mm fuchsia crystal onto the wire.

17 **Form** another simple loop of the same size, as close to the bead as possible. Congrats! You've created a bead link.

18 Using your wire cutters, **cut** the excess wire from the end of the bead link.

19 **Repeat** steps 15–18 to create a second bead link.

20 **Affix** one end of one of your bead links to the 7mm soldered jump ring you attached to the body of the bookmark.

21 **Attach** the second loop of this bead link to one of the two remaining 7mm soldered jump rings.

22 **Repeat** steps 20 and 21 to attach the second bead link to the other end of the bookmark.

23 **Split up** the flower and leaf dangles into two equal piles, each with three leaf dangles and 13 flower dangles.

24 Using 4mm jump rings, **attach** all the flower and leaf dangles in one of the piles onto the two 7mm jump rings at one end of the bookmark, distributing them as evenly as possible.

25 **Repeat** step 24 on the other end of the bookmark.

Variation

Clip Art

by Tracy Gritter

If you're more of a "book clip" type, don't despair. You can still integrate your beading with your reading with a crafty wire clip. To construct, start with 15 in of 18-gauge wire. Form one end of the wire into a spiral, and then form a heart shape. From there, twirl away, adding a few beads as you go. Be sure the wire crosses itself in a few places so the clip can grab onto the page. (Incidentally, this piece also makes for a fabulous paper clip.)

◆ Part Three ◆

Additional Information

Appendix A

◆◆◆

The Resourceful Beader

Look, as thorough as I've been, I'd be lying if I said I had taught you everything there is to know about beading in this one measly book. To make up for any failings on my part, I've included this nifty appendix of resources. On these pages you'll find pointers to various books, magazines, Web sites, and the like that will instruct and inspire you.

Books

Half of me wants to persuade you that my book is the only book you'll ever need. The other half of me knows that the first half is totally full of crap. Per my better half, here are some books, not written by me, that I heartily recommend:

- ◆ *Fashion Beading* by **Kim Ballor.** If you can't find a beading project you like among the 50 presented here, you're just being difficult.

- ◆ *Bead Girl: 25 Sparkly Beading Projects, from Toe Rings to Tiaras* by **Mikyla Bruder.** Technically written for girls ages 8 and up, this book has enough to keep adult-ish types interested, plus a supply packet with enough materials to make 10 projects. Besides, it has instructions for *tiaras*, for crying out loud. Who can resist?

- ◆ *The New! Beader's Companion* by **Jean Campbell and Judith Durant.** With all due respect to me and *my* book, this is *the* book to have if you're captivated by beading with seed beads using stitches like the peyote stitch, the brick stitch, the right-angle weave, and what have you. This handy reference steps you through these stitches and more. It doesn't include projects, but it does serve as an excellent reference for the seed beader.

- *Creating Extraordinary Beads from Ordinary Materials* **by Tina Casey.** People who like cooking from scratch will especially like this book, which demonstrates how to create your own beads using paper, glue, and a hollow cotton swab. (Foreword by MacGyver. Just kidding.)

- *Designer Style Jewelry: Techniques and Projects for Elegant Designs from Classic to Retro* **by Sherri Haab.** In addition to writing books geared for adults, Haab also writes books for kiddie crafters—and it shows in her ability to break down even the most complicated tasks into idiot-proof steps. If you're particularly craft-impaired, this may be the book for you.

- *All Wired Up* **by Mark Lareau.** First, the fact that a dude wrote this book clearly demonstrates that beading isn't just for chicks, whatever your roommate's obnoxious boyfriend might say. Second, it'll show you how to make some sweet spirally head pins, even if you've never picked up a pair of pliers. My only beef? The author includes a photo gallery of some especially cool pieces, but no instructions on how to make them.

- *Bead on a Wire* **by Sharilyn Miller.** If you're cheap, like me, you'll love the fact that, among other things, this book clearly illustrates how you can make your own jump rings, earring hooks, clasps, bead connectors, wire links, and the like.

- *The Beader's Palette: Rings, Necklaces, Bracelets, Ensembles, Earrings and Straps* **by Ondorisha.** Chock-full of lovely, delicate pieces that use gorgeous color schemes, this book will appeal to just about anyone, although it might not hurt to have a few projects under your belt before you take this title on.

- *The Impatient Beader* **by Margot Potter.** If you prefer gratification of the instant variety, then this is the book for you. It boasts more than 40 projects, plus variations, many of which you can toss together in less time than it takes to watch *Desperate Housewives.*

- *Making Designer Bead and Wire Jewelry: Techniques for Unique Designs and Handmade Findings* **by Tammy Powley.** If you're new to wirework, you'll appreciate this book's concise instructions and handy diagrams. Like *Bead on a Wire,* this book outlines how to make your own findings, and includes several nifty projects. Moderator of the About.com jewelry-making site, Powley clearly knows her stuff.

- *Bead Fantasies* **by Takako Samejima.** If I was on *Survivor* and was allowed but one beading-related book (in addition to my own, natch), it would be this one—provided, of course, I was also permitted to have all the supplies required to complete the featured projects. Simply put, Samejima's designs are gorgeous.

- *Bead Fantasies II: More Beautiful, Easy-to-Make Jewelry* **by Takako Samejima.** Going back to that whole *Survivor* scenario, if I could bring *two* beading-related books (again, in addition to my own), this would be my second, hands-down.

- *Beautiful Beading: Designs for Handmade Beads, Jewelry and Decorative Objects* **by Sara Withers.** If you're relatively new to beading, and still working to pin down your personal jewelry style, this might be a good place to start. This book is designed to introduce you to a variety of beading techniques as opposed to delving deeply into any one.

♦ ***The Encyclopedia of Beading Techniques*** **by Sara Withers and Stephanie Burnham.** This book, which, as its title suggests, details a variety of beading techniques, is a handy reference for new and experienced beaders alike.

Print Magazines

If you're looking for a steady stream of project ideas and tutorials, then beading magazines are the way to go. Most of the magazines listed here are published on a bi-monthly basis.

♦ ***Art Jewelry Magazine*** **(www.artjewelrymag.com).** Detailed step-by-step instructions, photographs, and helpful tips will help you re-create the pieces featured in this magazine. Projects aren't limited to beadwork; you'll discover other jewelry-making techniques involving such materials as wire and metal, metal-infused and polymer clay, stone, glass, fiber, leather, enamel, lacquer, paint, and more. You'll also learn about various tools and products with which to expand your *oeuvre*.

♦ ***Bead & Button*** **(www.beadandbutton.com).** Crammed with projects, patterns, and tutorials, *Bead & Button* is *the* periodical for the dedicated beader. A gallery of beadwork submitted by readers will serve to inspire you. (Try to overlook the fact that a majority of the pieces seem to feature fairies or dogs, and just appreciate the unbelievable workmanship.) In addition to its regular bi-monthly issues, *Bead & Button* produces various special editions, including *Beading Basics: Stitches*; *Beading Basics: Color*; *Beading Basics: Your Perfect Look*; and *Chic & Easy Fashion Jewelry*.

♦ ***Bead Unique Magazine*** **(www.beaduniquemag.com).** Whether you're new to this whole beading thing or a seasoned vet, you'll find projects in *Bead Unique* to explore your craft. Easy-to-follow instructions and step-by-step photos make it painless. The magazine doesn't limit its scope to jewelry; you'll find projects for home décor and more.

♦ ***BeadStyle*** **(www.beadstylemag.com).** Published by the people who bring you *Bead & Button*, each issue of *BeadStyle* boasts step-by-step instructions for making jewelry that rivals anything you'll find at an upscale boutique. Regardless of your skill level, *BeadStyle* can help you craft your own beautiful pieces using a variety of materials.

♦ ***Beadwork*** **(www.interweave.com/bead).** Like *Bead & Button*, *Beadwork* serves as a fantastic source of inspiration and ideas, with step-by-step instructions for finishing a range of projects.

♦ ***Jewelry Crafts Magazine*** **(www.jewelrycraftsmag.com).** In *Jewelry Crafts Magazine*, you'll be able to feed your addiction to jewelry-making with how-tos for beading, lampworking, silversmithing—even for making glass cane.

♦ ***Lapidary Journal*** **(www.lapidaryjournal.com).** If your goal is to expand your jewelry-making repertoire beyond beading, take a peek at an issue of *Lapidary Journal*. You'll find great articles, jewelry-making workshops, gorgeous photos, and a calendar of gem shows worldwide. Of particular help on the magazine's Web site is its list of bead societies across the globe, which you can use to connect with fellow beaders.

- ***Simply Beads* (www.simplybeadsmagazine.com).** Pretty projects, practical tips, and money-saving ideas abound in *Simply Beads*. In addition to discovering some great jewelry pieces, you'll also find loads of ideas for beaded projects for the home. If you have a short attention span, you'll appreciate the simplicity of the ideas presented here.
- ***Step by Step Beads* (www.stepbystepbeads.com).** Brought to you by the editors of *Lapidary Journal*, each issue of *Step by Step Beads* features as many as 20 beading projects. You'll also learn how to master techniques that the magazine deems essential.
- ***Step by Step Wire Jewelry* (www.stepbystepwire.com).** This quarterly magazine, also from the editors of *Lapidary Journal*, is packed with projects for wire jewelry-makers of all skill levels. You'll learn how to make great jewelry on the cheap using wire, stones, findings, beads, gems, and jigs.

Web Sites

God only knows what people did before the Internet. Life without eBay or without online shopping of any kind—I just can't think about it. In this section, I'll show you how you can harness the power of the Internet to feed your need to bead.

Online Tutorials, Instructions, Information, Etc.

Not surprisingly, the Internet has a wealth of beading-related resources. Here are a few sites featuring tutorials, instructions, patterns, projects, or other nifty tidbits. Some are from bona-fide companies, while others are provided by regular workaday types.

- About.com Beadwork (beadwork.about.com)
- About.com Jewelry Making (jewelrymaking.about.com)
- All About Beading (www.allaboutbeading.com)
- Bead and Button Magazine Basic Techniques (www.beadandbutton.com; click Basic Techniques under Online Content)
- Bead Stringing Projects by Patrice (pmegio.com/index.html)
- Bead Wrangler (www.beadwrangler.com)
- Bead-Patterns.com (www.bead-patterns.com)
- Beadage (www.beadage.net)
- BeadBugle.com (www.beadbugle.com)
- Beaded Impressions Tutorials (www.abeadstore.com; click Onsite Tutorials)
- BeadieFriends.com Beading Instructions (www.beadiefriends.com; click Beading Instructions)
- Beading Life (www.beadinglife.com)
- Beads, Baubles & Jewels Projects (www.beadsbaublesandjewels.com; click Projects)

- Beadwork Magazine Projects (www.interweave.com; click Projects & Articles)
- Fire Mountain Gems Beading How-Tos (www.firemountaingems.com/beading_howtos)
- HGTV Bead Projects (www.hgtv.com; click the Decorating tab, choose Crafts, and click Beads)
- Lapidary Journal Projects (www.lapidaryjournal.com/stepbystep)
- Michaels Arts and Crafts: Beads (www.michaels.com; click the Bead tab)
- Pattern Index (www.geocities.com/craftplus2000/1FreeIndex.html)
- Rings & Things Online Jewelry Projects (www.rings-things.com; click Projects)
- Robyn's Bead Page (www.geocities.com/robynl_4/index.html)
- Tutorials by Connie Fox (www.conniefox.com; click Education)
- WigJig's Jewelry-Making Tutorials for Beginners (www.wigjig.com; click Beginners Instructions)

Online Beading and Jewelry Supply Stores

First things first: where to buy stuff online. I have compiled a list here of only those beading-related Web sites that really make me drool. (It goes without saying you can find loads of bead supplies on eBay, so I won't say it.)

- Amonite Jewelry and Beads (www.eAmonite.com)
- ArtGemsInc.com (artgemsinc.com)
- Ball Chain Manufacturing Co. Inc. (www.ballchain.com)
- The Bead Goes On (www.beadgoeson.com)
- The Bead Hut (www.thebeadhut.com)
- The Bead Monkey (www.thebeadmonkey.com)
- The Bead Shop (www.beadshop.com)
- The Beadin' Path (www.beadinpath.com)
- Beads 925 (www.beads925.com)
- Beadworks (www.beadworks.com/us)
- Bella Venetian Beads (www.bellavenetianbeads.com)
- Bokamo Designs (www.bokamodesigns.com)
- Bonita Creations (www.bonitacreations.com)
- Brightlings Beads (www.brightlingsbeads.com)
- Charm Factory (www.charmfactory.com)
- Chelsea's Beads (www.chelseasbeads.com)

- ◆ Eclectica Beads (www.eclecticabeads.com)
- ◆ Elephant Eye Beads (www.elephanteyebeads.com)
- ◆ Fire Mountain Gems and Beads (www.firemountaingems.com)
- ◆ Foxden Designs (www.foxdendesigns.com)
- ◆ FusionBeads.com (www.fusionbeads.com)
- ◆ A Grain of Sand (www.agrainofsand.com)
- ◆ GiftsJoy.com (www.giftsjoy.com)
- ◆ Heather Trimlett (www.heathertrimlett.com)
- ◆ House of Gems (www.houseofgems.com)

> ## Rio Grande
>
> While technically not an online storefront, Rio Grande, which sells jewelry supplies through its catalogs, deserves a mention. Put simply, if an item relates in any way to the production of jewelry of any kind, Rio Grande carries it. Indeed, simply flipping through any of the tome-sized catalogs Rio Grande issues is an education unto itself; you'll discover goodies you never knew existed—but that you suddenly can't live without. To order your Rio Grande catalogs, visit www.riogrande.com. (Note that each catalog costs $10, but the fact that you'll receive a $10 gift certificate toward your purchase makes for offsetting penalties.)

- ◆ Jewelry and Bead Supply (www.jewelryandbeadsupply.com)
- ◆ JewelrySupply.com (www.jewelrysupply.com)
- ◆ Kemayab Imports (www.kibeads.com)
- ◆ Latitudes Trading Company (www.latitudestrading.com)
- ◆ Le Beaderie (www.lebeaderie.com)
- ◆ Lillypilly Designs (lillypillydesigns.com)
- ◆ M&J Trimming (www.mjtrim.com)
- ◆ Mr. Bead (www.mrbead.com)
- ◆ Natural Touch Beads (www.naturaltouchbeads.com)
- ◆ Nina Designs (www.ninadesigns.com)
- ◆ One Bead at a Time (www.onebead.com)
- ◆ Ornamenta (www.ornamentea.com)
- ◆ Pacific Silverworks (pacificsilverworks.com)
- ◆ Primitive Earth Beads (www.primitiveearthbeads.com)
- ◆ Saki Silver (www.sakisilver.com)
- ◆ Shiana (www.shiana.com)
- ◆ Shipwreck Beads (www.shipwreckbeads.com)
- ◆ Star's Clasps (starsclasps.com)

- ♦ StonesNSilver.com (www.stonesnsilver.com)
- ♦ TA Pearl Stone (www.tapearlstone.com)
- ♦ TibetanBeads.com (tibetanbeads.com)
- ♦ Tika Imports (www.tikaimports.com)
- ♦ Venetian Bead Shop (www.venetianbeadshop.com)

Brick-and-Mortar Bead Shops

Rather than list the 34-gazillion bead shops that dot the Earth, I figured I'd save some trees by citing a Web site that you can use to quickly and easily locate a shop in your area: BeadShopFinder.com (www.beadshopfinder.com). For example, when I type my ZIP code, BeadShopFinder returns a list of 10 shops in my area (which, in case you're wondering, is Indianapolis)—including my two favorites, Boca Loca Beads and Bead Angels—with links to contact information.

Bead Shows

Bead shops are great, don't get me wrong. But the same impulse that drove the inventor of the shopping mall to consolidate numerous stores under one roof is alive and well among organizers of bead shows. At any of the shows listed here, you'll encounter dozens—even hundreds—of beading suppliers. Some of these shows are traveling affairs, touching down in myriad cities nationwide; others are an annual deal occurring once yearly at the same location. For more information about a show, and to find out if it's making a stop near you, visit its Web site.

- ♦ **Ayla's Wonderful World of Beads (www.awwbshow.com).** Top bead vendors from around the world provide a wide selection of high-quality freshwater pearls, gemstones, art glass, sterling silver, seed beads, findings, and beading supplies.
- ♦ **The Bead and Button Show (www.beadandbuttonshow.com).** Touted as the world's biggest bead show, this annual weeklong celebration of the bead boasts classes taught by world-renowned instructors, nearly 350 vendors hawking beading supplies and finished jewelry, and hordes of fellow beaders.
- ♦ **Bead Fest (www.beadfest.com).** This year, two Bead Fest events are scheduled, each with more than 100 classes and over 200 vendors—all devoted to beading! Even if you're not interested in expanding your mind, you can always expand your bead collection. Bead Fest is a production of *Step by Step Beads* and *Lapidary Journal*.
- ♦ **The Bead Market (www.thebeadmarket.net).** For a wide selection of gemstones, pearls, buttons, glass beads, lampwork, seed beads, tools, and jewelry, check out the Bead Market. Its Texas locations include Fort Worth, San Antonio, Houston, and Dallas; the show also stops in Arkansas and Louisiana.

- **The Bead Renaissance Show (www.beadshow.com).** With 10 events on the docket, primarily in the American West, the Bead Renaissance Show caters to both retail and wholesale beaders. You'll find bead artists, merchants, and traders with such goodies as finished jewelry; beads of the ancient, vintage, and contemporary variety; gemstone beads; and buttons. Even better, admission is free.

- **The Down the Street Bead Show (www.thedownthestreetbeadshow.com).** If you live in Florida, Georgia, South Carolina, or North Carolina, keep an ear to the ground for this bead show. You're guaranteed to find vintage glass beads, Austrian crystal, freshwater pearls, sterling silver beads and pendants, furnace glass beads, gemstone beads, marcasite beads, lampwork beads, Italian glass beads, findings, finished jewelry, and more. Although events in this series are smaller in size than in some other shows, they promise superior-quality beads.

- **Gem Faire (www.gemfaire.com).** Established in 1989, Gem Faire, which conducts a ballpark figure of 40 shows each year, offers the finest in gemstones, beads, minerals, fossils, meteorites, finished pieces, and lapidary equipment—and at prices that won't break the bank. Classes are available for the curious.

- **The Gem, Jewelry, and Bead Show (www.frankcoxproductions.com).** With nearly two dozen events annually, the Gem, Jewelry, and Bead Show caters to beaders in Florida, Georgia, and North Carolina.

- **The Innovative Beads Expo (www.innovativebeadsexpo.com).** The Innovative Beads Expo boasts nearly two shows each month, each with myriad quality merchants and, when possible, classes.

- **Intergalactic Bead Shows (www.beadshows.com).** Thousands of beaders attend events by Intergalactic Bead Shows each year, all interested in the amazing variety of emeralds, rubies, freshwater pearls, and other beads.

- **The International Bead Expo (www.beadexpo.com).** This bead show includes a bazaar that boasts more than 150 booths selling beads, findings, tools, books, videotapes, jewelry, and textiles. In addition, first-rate instructors conduct workshops on a variety of beading-related topics.

- **The Whole Bead Show (www.wholebead.com).** If you're looking to be overwhelmed by choices, check out the Whole Bead Show, which touches down in roughly a dozen cities each year. It features beads made from precious and semi-precious gems, silver and gold, vintage and contemporary glass and crystal, plastic, and natural materials. In addition, you'll discover findings, charms, pendants, and even some pre-made jewelry.

Appendix B

◆◆◆

Best Laid Plans

Some of us, and I'm not naming names, like to wing it, designing our beaded pieces as we go. Others like to plan out their pieces beforehand. If you're among the prissy-pants planners, this appendix is for you. Here you'll find nifty tools to help you map out your stitch pieces, guesstimate the length of your baubles, and otherwise take the fun out of things.

Plot Points

If, say, you're looking to construct a replica of the Sistine Chapel ceiling with 15/0 delicas, you'll probably want to plot out your design on paper first. Just what kind of paper you use, however, depends on what stitch you plan to employ. If you've opted for the square stitch or the ladder stitch, then plain-old run-of-the-mill graph paper, which you can filch from the math nerd of your choice, does the trick. (Graph paper also works in a pinch for plotting out your right-angle weave pieces, although using specialized right-angle weave paper is a bit easier.) If, however, you plan to construct your homage to Michelangelo using the brick or peyote stitch, you'll need special paper in which the squares in the grid are offset. These sample sheets, which you can copy to your big heart's content, are just the ticket. Use the graph paper on the next page for peyote stitch and brick stitch. (If you plan to stitch the design with a brick stitch, rotate the paper 90 degrees.) Plotting out your right-angle weave pieces on the graph paper on page 199 can make your life as easy as Samantha on *Sex and the City*.

Of course, because the seed beads used to stitch pieces are available in a variety of sizes, the dimension of the piece you've meticulously plotted on paper will depend on the size of the seed beads you use. The following table should help you figure out a rough estimate. (Note that just to confuse matters, Japanese seed beads are sized slightly differently from Czech seed beads.)

Czech Seed Beads

Bead Size	Beads Per Inch	Bead Size	Beads Per Inch
16/0	28	10/0	16
14/0	25	9/0	15
13/0	24	8/0	14
12/0	21	6/0	9
11/0	18		

Japanese Seed Beads

Bead Size	Beads Per Inch
14/0	27
11/0	17
8/0	11
6/0	7

Measure Up

Has this ever happened to you? You buy a strand of yummy Czech crystals. You bring them home. They intermingle with the rest of your vast bead collection. Suddenly, however, you can't remember whether they're 2mm or 4mm, which means you don't know whether they're the right size for the kick-ass pattern you just found online. In the immortal words of Keanu Reeves in *Speed*, "What do you do? What. Do. You. Do?" *Answer:* You compare one of the beads with the drawings in the following size charts. Problem solved.

Seed Bead Sizes

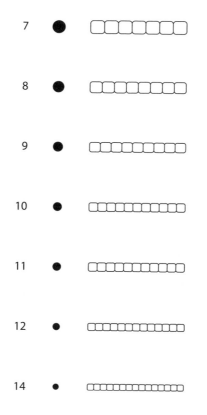

Note the size range in seed beads.

Circle Bead Sizes in Millimeters

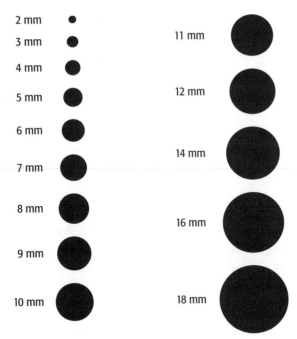

2 mm
3 mm
4 mm
5 mm
6 mm
7 mm
8 mm
9 mm
10 mm

11 mm
12 mm
14 mm
16 mm
18 mm

Oval Bead Sizes in Millimeters

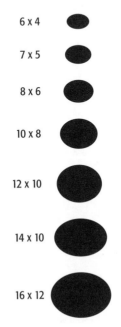

6 x 4
7 x 5
8 x 6
10 x 8
12 x 10
14 x 10
16 x 12

Speaking of measuring, you probably noticed that bead sizes are typically given in millimeters. If you're morally opposed to using the metric system, you can convert those millimeters to inches using this chart. (Actually, the chart converts centimeters to inches so you don't get eyestrain looking at millimeters.) Just remember: One centimeter equals 10 millimeters.

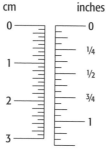

Centimeters/ Inch Gauge

Convert those pesky millimeters to inches.

Obviously, the length of your piece plays an important role. If you're making a bracelet, you probably want it to run 7 inches or so. If you're stringing a rope you plan to saucily toss over your shoulder, you'll want it to be 48 inches, give or take. For help nailing your numbers, refer to the following guide.

Standard Bracelet, Anklet, and Necklace Lengths

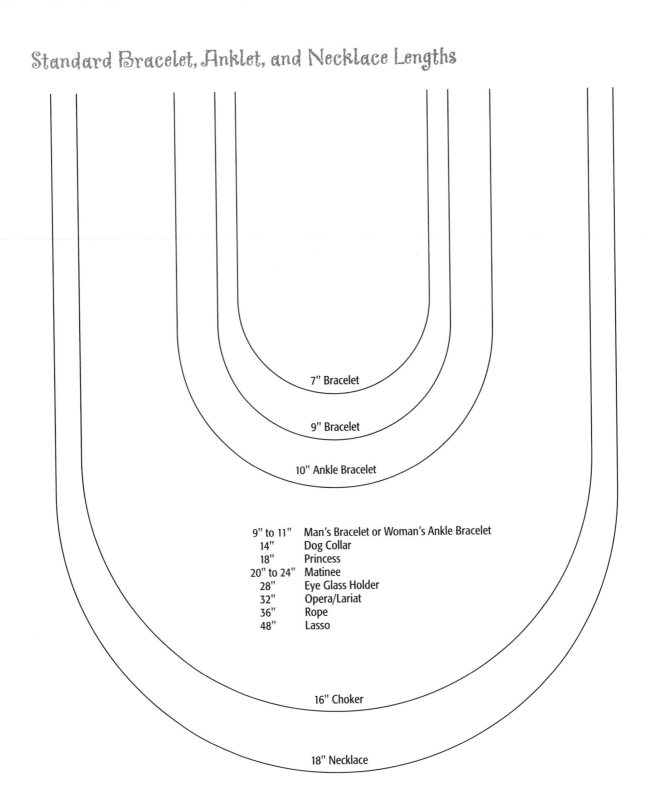

7" Bracelet

9" Bracelet

10" Ankle Bracelet

9" to 11"	Man's Bracelet or Woman's Ankle Bracelet
14"	Dog Collar
18"	Princess
20" to 24"	Matinee
28"	Eye Glass Holder
32"	Opera/Lariat
36"	Rope
48"	Lasso

16" Choker

18" Necklace

If you plan to work with wire, you'll undoubtedly encounter wire of various gauges. To help you figure out which gauges are thin and which are thick, check out this diagram.

Know Your Gauges

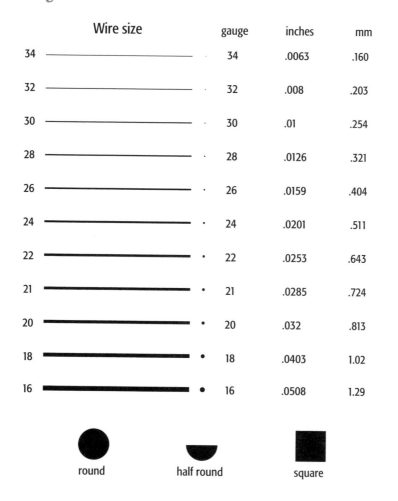

Wire size	gauge	inches	mm
34	34	.0063	.160
32	32	.008	.203
30	30	.01	.254
28	28	.0126	.321
26	26	.0159	.404
24	24	.0201	.511
22	22	.0253	.643
21	21	.0285	.724
20	20	.032	.813
18	18	.0403	1.02
16	16	.0508	1.29

round   half round   square

Appendix C

◆◆◆

Cheat Sheet

ook, don't feel like an idiot if you can't remember the difference between a wafer and a donut. (Mmm. Donut. Dammit! I'm hungry *again*!) It's a lot to take in! Use this appendix as a handy reference to help you keep it all straight.

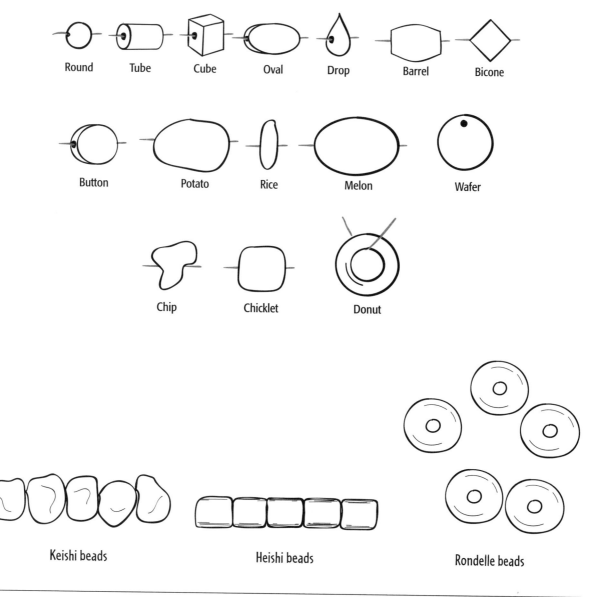

Round Tube Cube Oval Drop Barrel Bicone

Button Potato Rice Melon Wafer

Chip Chicklet Donut

Keishi beads   Heishi beads   Rondelle beads

Bead shapes at a glance.

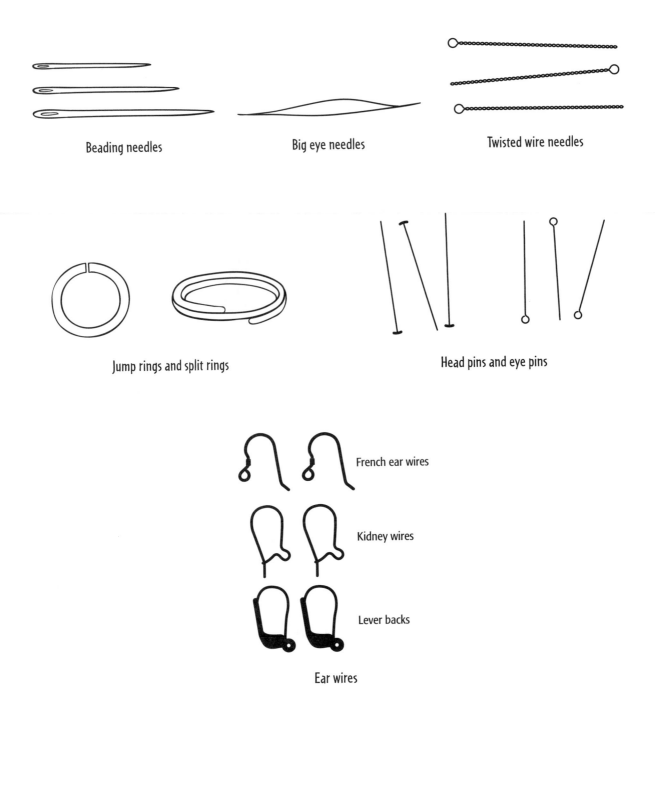

Beading needles

Big eye needles

Twisted wire needles

Jump rings and split rings

Head pins and eye pins

French ear wires

Kidney wires

Lever backs

Ear wires

Bead caps

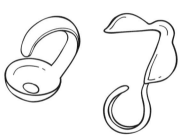

Clamshells and bead tips

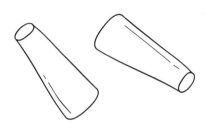

Cones

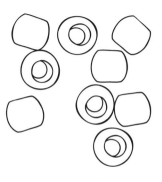

Crimp beads

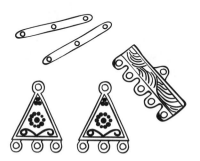

Connectors, separator bars,
and end bars

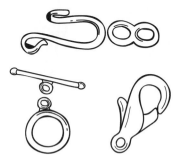

Lobster-claw clasp, toggle clasp,
and S-hook clasp

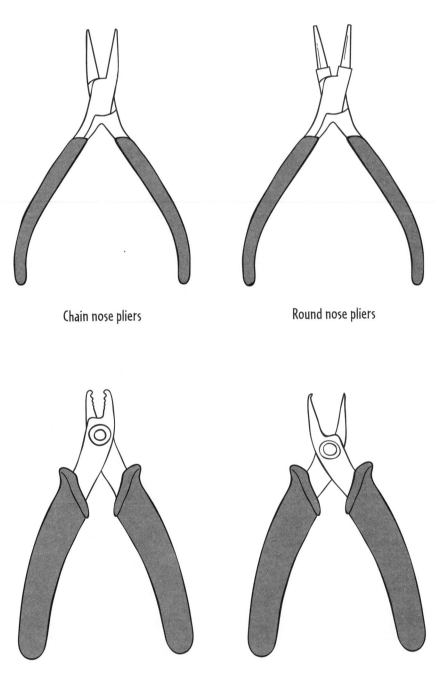

Chain nose pliers

Round nose pliers

Crimping pliers

Split ring pliers

Appendix D

◆◆◆

I Wish I Could Kit You

If your budget is more "tramp" than "Trump," you're probably wondering which tools and materials are *absolutely essential* for your beading kit, and which you can overlook for now. Allow me to enlighten you.

The Bead Stringer's Bare Minimum

If bead stringing's your bag, first decide whether you want to use traditional thread, such as the nylon or silk variety, or beading wire, as in Beadalon or SoftFlex. If you opt for beading wire, you'll need this kit:

- ◆ Bead mat
- ◆ Beads
- ◆ Beading wire
- ◆ Crimp beads
- ◆ Clasps
- ◆ Wire cutters
- ◆ Crimping pliers

If you prefer the more traditional thread, you'll need a slightly different type of kit:

- Bead mat
- Beads
- Silk thread, nylon thread, or FireLine
- Beeswax or thread conditioner
- Sharp beading scissors
- Needles (these can be beading needles, sharps, big-eye needles, or twisted wire needles)
- Needle threader
- Corsage pin (if you plan to add knots between the beads)
- Clamshells or bead tips
- Clasps
- Super Glue

The Bead Stitcher's Skeleton Crew

The bead stitcher's kit is similar to the bead stringer's:

- Bead mat
- Beads (usually seed beads)
- Nylon thread or FireLine
- Beeswax or thread conditioner
- Sharp beading scissors
- Beading needles
- Needle threader
- Clasps
- Super Glue

The Wireworker's Lower Limits

"Wirework" is a broad term, ranging from a person who uses a head pin to form an earring dangle to a person who forms a life-size wireframe replica of the World's Largest Ball of String with bead accents. Regardless of which variety of wireworker you are, you'll at the very least need these items on hand:

- ◆ Bead mat
- ◆ Wire
- ◆ Beads
- ◆ Chain nose pliers
- ◆ Round nose pliers
- ◆ Wire cutters (if you plan to work with memory wire, you should also buy cutters designed specifically for that purpose)

Initial Findings

In addition, regardless of what type of beading you want to do—stringing, stitching or wirework—you'll want to keep some basic findings on hand:

- ◆ Head pins
- ◆ Earring wires
- ◆ Jump rings
- ◆ Clasps

Designer Bios

Charissa Brannen Growing up near the coast of the Atlantic Ocean in Sanford, Maine, Charissa Brannen fell in love with design and fashion at an early age. Self-taught, she found her niche making jewelry. Brannen strives to make each of her pieces eclectic, unique, and innovative, and focuses on using inspirational blends of color, unusual silver findings, and stones with unique shapes and textures. Her silver-wrapping technique and unconventional vision are surpassed only by her commitment to quality and beauty. Brannen's goal is to continue to develop exciting and extraordinary pieces of wearable art.

Tracy Gritter and Denise Town In addition to co-founding Perfect Placement & Design, an interior decorating service, Tracy Gritter and Denise Town are principal partners of Gallery 116 (www.gallery116.com), a cozy and unique shop housed in an old bungalow that once served as the town hall in Fishers, Indiana. In addition to providing local artists with an opportunity to consign their wares, Gritter and Town sell their own creations, all of which reflect their quirky sense of design and zest for life.

Terri Hansen When Terri Hansen's husband accepted a 7-day-a-week night job, Hansen, who herself worked days, decided she needed a hobby, and hit upon making jewelry. In time, the self-described "genuine nutcase" began earning enough money selling her designs that she was able to quit her job—and spend time with her husband again!

Laury Henry Although Laury Henry, who has been a beader since the days of plastic pop-it beads, was born in Washington, D.C., she has called Spring, Texas, home since 1980. In addition to holding down a full-time accounting job, Henry works part-time as an instructor at Auntie's Beads in Old Town Spring. Although Henry is primarily self-taught, she did study metalsmithing at the University of Houston, and is certified in precious metal clay.

Rianne Keedy Heavily influenced by her OCD, Rianne Keedy was drawn to the tiny size and bright colors of seed beads about 3 years ago, when she may or may not have taken a crafts class with James Frey while visiting an inpatient rehabilitation facility.

Rachel Nelson-Smith Bead artist, teacher, and jewelry designer Rachel Nelson-Smith's work has been displayed at the Milpitas Museum, Santa Cruz Metro Center, and other locations in the California Bay Area and beyond. In addition, a number of her original projects have appeared in *Bead & Button Magazine*, including her "Crystal Mandala Necklace" in December 2005 (issue #70) and "Loop Hoop Earrings" in February 2006 (issue # 71). Since 1996, Nelson-Smith has taught basic to advanced classes in the San Francisco Bay Area and elsewhere around the United States. Residing in the beautiful Santa Cruz Mountains with her husband, Colin, and her bead collection, Nelson-Smith strives to hook other prospective beaders on her addiction.

Sonya Rhiver Illinois native Sonya Rhiver developed her love for jewelry—especially her grandmother's pieces—early in life. Although Rhiver began her career teaching elementary and junior high school, her hobby of experimenting with paper, paint, beads, and wire to make earrings soon pointed her in a different direction. After selling her pieces at craft fairs, Rhiver, in partnership with her mother, launched a jewelry business, Unique Accents Inc. (www.unique-accents.com).

Arturo Rodriguez Rodriguez, who hails from Peru, is a second-generation metal artist. Rodriguez created his first piece of jewelry at age 7; by age 12, he had gained enough experience and knowledge to open his own small shop. He continued perfecting his craft through high school, landing a job as a designer for a leading Peruvian jewelry company upon graduation. In 1995, Rodriguez transplanted himself to Bloomington, Indiana, where he frequently tutors students from the Indiana University School of Fine Arts. In addition to designing his own mixed-media pieces, Rodriguez teaches others at Indianapolis bead store Boca Loca Beads (where, incidentally, he met his wife, Tanya, who is a fellow jewelry designer and contributor to this book), and is currently working to produce a line of instructional materials.

Jari Sheese Sheese discovered her love of jewelry design when studying abroad in Peru, learning the ins and outs of the craft from street artisans. After blowing her savings, Sheese became an artisan herself, surviving off her earnings. Upon her return to the United States, Sheese figured she'd continue making jewelry as a hobby; in fact, it took over her life. After making the rounds at art fairs, Sheese launched her own bead shop, Boca Loca Beads (www.bocalocabeadsinc.com); in addition to teaching glass-bead making classes in the shop's studio, Sheese enjoys traveling the globe in search of unique and beautiful beads for her customers.

Olga Skurat Moscow native Olga Skurat earned a degree in interior design before switching her focus to jewelry design—and it shows in her knack for mixing colors. Now a resident of Indianapolis, Skurat teaches a series of classes at Boca Loca Beads, where she is so popular with her customers she actually has her own groupies.

Amy Swenson Swenson learned to crochet when she was still little enough to make blankets for her dolls. She promptly forgot everything about needlework until she turned 23, when she suddenly fell back in love with the idea of creating fabric. Since 2003, Swenson has developed and distributed her own line of original patterns for knitting and crochet, IndiKnits (www.indiknits.com), which can be found in more than 100 shops across North America. Although *Not Your Mama's Beading* is Swenson's first foray into beadwork, she is thrilled to have authored *Not Your Mama's Crochet,* and to have had knitting and crochet patterns appear in books including *Big Girl Knits, Knit Wit, Stitch 'n Bitch Nation,* and *Knitting for Dogs*. Aside from designing, Amy can be found in her fiber arts shop, Make One Yarn Studio (www.make1yarns.com) in Calgary, Alberta, where she and her partner are the proud humans of three cats who, thankfully, leave the yarn alone.

Tanya Tegmeyer-Rodriguez The self-taught Tanya Tegmeyer-Rodriguez began making jewelry in 1999, using magazines and library books to learn the ropes. By 2000, she had discovered that her passion was seed-bead weaving. Since 2004, Tegmeyer-Rodriguez has worked and taught at Boca Loca Beads (where, incidentally, she met her husband and fellow contributor Arturo Rodriguez). Tegmeyer-Rodriguez, whose "Bohemian Rouge" was featured in the book *500 Beaded Objects*, lives in Bloomington, Indiana with her husband, her cat, and her Chihuahua.

Danielle Tooley Danielle lives in Indianapolis and has been beading for over 2 years. The former high school English teacher turned beader is mostly self-taught but has been involved in the arts much of her life. She sells her pieces through private shows and by word of mouth. She also uses her pieces and talent as a means of ministering to people in her church and community. She is married to a wonderful and tolerant husband; they have three beautiful children.

Barbara Walling Walling invented her beautiful beaded bottles a few years ago, after inheriting a box of old buttons, beads, and junk jewelry from an aunt who kept *everything*. Originally, Walling made her pieces for friends, but quickly realized she'd need more friends if she wanted to keep making the bottles. Instead, she began selling them under the guise BarbWire. Walling also fashions mobiles and wind chimes from old silverware and kitchen utensils. In her "real life," Walling is a nurse, and frequently pilfers empty vaccine vials for her craft projects.

Connie Weber After working as an RN for 28 years, Indianapolis resident Connie Weber decided in 2002 that she was ready for a change. By then, she'd enjoyed beading as a hobby for 8 years; opening her own bead shop, Bead Angels, was the natural thing to do. Weber especially enjoys working with seed beads, and teaches several classes on various techniques to her customers. Her nursing skills come in handy when her students prick themselves with their beading sharps.

Index

◆◆◆

pony. *See* seed beads
potato, 19, 207
precious, 18
resin, 18
rice, 19, 207
Rondelle, 20, 207
round, 19, 207
seed
    Czech seed beads, 200
    Japanese seed
      beads, 200
    overview, 18
    for stitching, 39
semi-precious, 18
shapes of, 19–20
sizes of, 19–20, 200
snail-shell, 11–12
spiritual purpose of, 13
stitching
    adding clasps to stitched
      piece, 54–55
    beaded rings, 141–143
    brick stitch, 44
    buttons, 109–110
    daisy chain stitch,
      47–48
    feeding thread, 52–54
    fixing errors, 54
    flat peyote stitch, 41–43
    hair comb or barrettes,
      149–150
    ladder stitch, 49–50
    right angle weave,
      50–52
    spiked bracelet,
      119–123
    square stitch, 45–47
    stopper bead, 40
stringing
    anklets, 92–105
    attaching clasp, 36–37
    beaded bookmark,
      183–185
    cell-phone strap,
      160–161
    designing, 33–35

pushpins, 176
rings, 136–137
tools for, 35
watches, 88–90
tube, 19, 207
type of, 16–18
used as currency, 12
use of in African tribes, 10
wafer, 19, 207
white shell, 12
wood, 18
bead shows, 195–196
bead stitcher's kit, 212
beeswax, 21, 40
belts, 12–13, 153
beryl, 17
bicone beads, 19, 207
big eye needles, 23–24, 208
big ring project, 136–137
binding, cuff ends, 113–115
boards, bead, 34
books, 189–191
bobby pins, 150
bone beads, 18
book clips, 185
bookmarks, 183–185
bottles, 173–174
bouquet earrings, 147
bouquet ring project
    overview, 144
    steps in making, 144–147
    variations, 147
bracelets
    beadcheting, 106–108
    beaded, 137
    clasps for, 122
    dangling, 74, 117–118
    leather, 117–118
    made by Native American,
      12–13
    spiked
      attaching one end of
        clasp, 122
      base, 119–120
      crystal spikes, 120–121
      filling gaps, 121

overview, 119
    reinforcing, 122
    variations, 123–126
    standard lengths for, 204
    using buttons, 109–110
branches, tiara, 166
brick stitch, 44, 197
button beads, 19, 207
buttons, bracelet using, 109–110

C

calottes, 26
caps, bead, 26–27, 209
cards
    credit cards, necklace made
      with, 67–69
    place-card holders, 169–170
Catholic Church, 8, 9
ceiling fan pull, 177–179
cell-phone strap, 160–161
cement, 28
chain nose pliers, 29, 210
chains, 22, 179
chandelier earrings project
    overview, 132
    steps in making, 132–135
    variations, 135
charms
    bag charms, 159
    project using, 73–74
chevron beads, 10
chiclet beads, 19, 207
child tiara, 167
Chinese glass beads, 11
chip beads, 19, 207
chokers, 105, 108
circle bead sizes, 202
clamshells, 26, 209
clasps
    adding to stitched piece,
      54–55
    anklet, 104–105

pins
- bobby pins, 150
- corsage pin, 39
- eye pins, 25, 208
- hatpins, 176
- head pins, 25, 208
- lollipop head pin, 59
- pushpins, 176
- spiral-shaped head pin, 59
- stickpins, 176

rings
- beaded ring band, 142
- beaded table rings, 175
- bead stringing, 136–137
- bouquet ring, 144–147
- jump rings, 25, 88–89, 208
- key ring, 158–159
- napkin rings, 175
- nest ring, 138–140
- overview, 25
- split rings, 25, 208
- star showcased in, 86
- table rings, 175
- tipple rings, 171
- triangular jump rings, 88–89
- separator bars, 27, 209

FireLine, 21
five-pointed star pendant, 75–76, 80–81
flat peyote stitch, 41–43
flower dangles, 184
frames, 170
French ear wires, 26, 208
fringe, adding to anklet, 96–101

G

gauges, 204
gauge wire, 165

glass beads
- Chinese, 11
- Egyptian, 8
- history of, 8
- Indian, 8
- pressed, 18
- Roman, 8
glassmakers, 9
glue, 28
graph paper, 197
grunge, 15

H

hair clips, 149–150
hair comb, 149–150
hatpins, 176
head pins, 25, 208
headwear
- barrettes, 149–150
- lollipop head pin, 59
- tiara project
  - adding twisted branches, 165–167
  - body of tiara, 162–163
  - covering front, 163–165
  - overview, 162
  - variations, 167
healing stones, 17
heishi beads, 19, 207
holes, drilling, 23
hoop earrings, 128
horn beads, 18

I

ID badges, 155
inches, converting into millimeters, 203
Indian glass beads, 8
Islamic beads, 8

J

Japanese seed beads, 200
jeweler's cement, 28
jewelry overview, 13–14
jig, 29
jump rings, 25, 88–89, 208

K

Keishi beads, 207
Keishi pearls, 19
key ring, 158–159
kidney wires, 26, 208
kits, 211–212
knots, 39
Korea, 11

L

ladder stitch, 49–50, 197
lampwork beads, 16
lariats, 71–72
leaf dangles, 184
leashes, 182
leather cord
- overview, 21
- project using, 117–118
length of piece, 35
lever backs, 26, 208
Liberty Style, 14
link, 58
lollipop head pin, 59
loom, 47
loops
- simple loop, 57
- toggle loops, 157
- wrapped loops, 57–58
lopsided figure eight, 59
love beads, 15

M

magazines, print, 191–192
mandrel, ring, 30
mass-produced jewelry, 14
melon beads, 19, 207
memory wire, 22, 55
memory wire cutters, 28
metal beads, 17
metal wire, 22
methods, drawn, 9
Mexican beads, 11–12
millefiori bead, 10
Millimeter/Inch Gauge, 203
mistakes, fixing, 54
monofilament, 21

N

napkin rings, 175
navel-grazing necklace, 66
necklaces
    ball chains, 179
    made by Native American,
        12–13
    navel-grazing, 66
    standard lengths for, 204
needles
    big eye, 23–24, 208
    for stitching, 40
    threading, 24
    twisted wire, 24, 208
nest ring, 138–140
"New Look" design, 15
niobium wire, 22
North American beads, 12
nylon thread, 20

O

odd-count flat peyote stitch,
    42–43
oval beads, 19, 202, 207

P

paper, graph, 197
paper clips, 185
patterns, 53
pearls, Keishi, 19
pendants, 75–76, 80–81
petroleum-based beeswax, 21
peyote stitch, 197
picture frames, 170
pins
    bobby pins, 150
    corsage pin, 39
    eye pins, 25, 208
    hatpins, 176
    head pins, 25, 208
    lollipop head pin, 59
    pushpins, 176
    spiral-shaped head pin, 59
    stickpins, 176
place-card holders, 169–170
planning designs, 197
plastic snack trays, 32–33
plastic stoppers, 26
pliers
    chain nose, 29, 210
    crimping, 30, 37, 210
    round nose, 29, 210
    split ring, 30, 210
polymer beads, 17
pony beads. *See* seed beads
potato beads, 19, 207
precious beads, 18
pressed glass beads, 18
pulls
    ceiling fan pull, 177–178
    fan pull, 177–178
    zipper pulls, 154–155
pushpins, 176

Q

Queen Victoria, 13

R

reamer, 23
recycling, 173–174
resin beads, 18
ribbons
    overview, 22
    project using, 64–66
    stitching beads onto, 153
rice beads, 19, 207
right angle weave, 50–52
ring mandrel, 30
rings
    beaded ball ring, 140–143
    beaded ring band, 142
    beaded table rings, 175
    big ring project, 136–137
    bouquet ring project
        overview, 144
        steps in making,
            144–147
        variations, 147
    jump rings, 25, 88–89, 208
    key ring, 158–159
    napkin rings, 175
    nest ring, 138–140
    overview, 25
    split rings, 25, 208
    star showcased in, 86
    table rings, 175
    tipple rings, 171–172
    triangular jump rings, 88–89
Roman glass beads, 8
Rondelle beads, 20, 207
round beads, 19, 207
round nose pliers, 29, 210
Russian Revolution, 14

S

satin cord, 21–22
scalloping edges, 94
scissors, 28

About the Author

Kate Shoup Welsh During the course of her career, Kate Shoup Welsh has written or co-written several books and a screenplay. When not writing, Kate loves to ski (she was once nationally ranked) and ride her motorcycle, and she plays a mean game of 9-ball. Kate lives in Indianapolis with her husband, daughter, dog, and cat.

Notes

Notes

Notes